Survival

Survival

*Radical Spiritual Practices
for Trauma Survivors*

Karen O'Donnell

scm press

© Karen O Donnell 2024

Published in 2024 by SCM Press
Editorial office
3rd Floor, Invicta House,
110 Golden Lane,
London EC1Y 0TG, UK

www.scmpress.co.uk

SCM Press is an imprint of Hymns Ancient & Modern Ltd
(a registered charity)

Hymns Ancient & Modern® is a registered trademark of
Hymns Ancient & Modern Ltd
13A Hellesdon Park Road, Norwich,
Norfolk NR6 5DR, UK

All rights reserved. No part of this publication may be reproduced,
stored in a retrieval system, or transmitted,
in any form or by any means, electronic, mechanical,
photocopying or otherwise, without the prior permission of
the publisher, SCM Press.

The author has asserted her right under the Copyright, Designs and
Patents Act 1988 to be identified as the Author of this Work
British Library Cataloguing in Publication data
A catalogue record for this book is available
from the British Library

Bible quotations marked NLT are from the New Living Translation,
copyright © 1996, 2004, 2015 by Tyndale House Foundation. Used by
permission of Tyndale House Publishers, Inc., Carol Stream, Illinois 60188.
All rights reserved.
All other Bible quotations are taken from the New Revised Standard
Version Updated Edition, copyright © 2021 National Council of the
Churches of Christ in the United States of America. Used by permission.
All rights reserved worldwide.

ISBN: 978-0-334-06503-6

Typeset by Regent Typesetting

Contents

Acknowledgements   vii

Introduction: Radical Spaces for Radical Love   1

1 The Post-Traumatic Remaking of the Self   8
2 The Practice of Unforgiveness   19
3 The Practice of Anger   31
4 The Practice of Hopelessness   43
5 The Practice of Taking Action   58
6 The Practice of Deconstruction   73
7 The Practice of Pleasure (yes, that kind of pleasure!)   87
8 The Practice of Rest   100
9 The Practice of Eating Good Food   112

Afterword: Keep on Surviving   125

Appendix: In the Sacred Pause – Liturgical Resources for Holy Saturday   129

Additional Material for 'In the Sacred Pause'   144

Index of Names and Subjects   149

For those who survive. Keep on surviving.

Acknowledgements

Most of this book was written after I had begun working at Westcott House in Cambridge and so I was settling into a new role and exploring a new part of the world. I have huge thanks for my colleagues at Westcott who are always supportive and excellent people to talk works in progress with. My students in Cambridge were also significant inspirations for this work as they continually asked wise and probing questions about what trauma survivors might do next. Many of my students are training to be priests and their pastoral interests were excellent prompts for me to think about how I might shape and frame this work. I hope this is a book they will have in their offices and that they will find inspiration within its pages for how they care for their parishes. I want to acknowledge the many trauma survivors I have encountered over the years who have been both encouraging and challenging. They have pushed me to think seriously about the embodied, spiritual and practical implications of the trauma theologies I have been writing. This book is an attempt at an answer to your questions.

I have particular thanks for people who have read chapters and helped me think through issues as I have written this book: Sarah Pritchard, Katie Cross, Scott Midson, Jenny Leith, Will Moore, Maureen Wright, Alison Gray, and the whole of my Theology and Trauma class. An extra special thank you goes to one of the groups in this class who produced such fantastic trauma-informed resources for Holy Saturday that I wanted to include them as an appendix in this volume to make them available to people: Ian Henderson, Mary Kilikidi, Claire Brocklesby and Dan Krawczyk. As always, I am grateful to my wonderful editor David Shervington and the whole team at SCM Press for their support and encouragement, especially as this book arrived a little later than planned. Finally, I want to thank my partner James for his continuous support and love that is always encouraging and comforting. Writing is hard but having this kind of support makes it possible and even enjoyable!

Introduction

Radical Spaces for Radical Love

I have been working in the field of trauma theology for more than a decade and regularly over that time people have responded to my work with the question 'So what?' Sometimes this is 'So what should I, as a Christian minister, therefore do or change within my ministry?' Other times, when I have talked about the process of post-traumatic remaking and the need to pay attention to the body within the process, the question has been 'So what can I, as a trauma survivor who is a Christian, do?' Both of these are, I think, really good questions and were the provocation I needed to think further about the implications of this work I have been doing, for the very real people with very real experiences to whom I was talking. I have spent time working on exploring the ways in which trauma challenges and transforms the way we think theologically but have not, until now, really articulated how a trauma survivor might work through the impact of this kind of theology. That is what I am doing in this book.

I wanted to pick up some of the challenging themes that trauma presents for theology and explore what that might mean for the trauma survivor who is seeking out their own remaking in the aftermath of trauma. As I have explored the relationship between trauma and theology, a number of key themes have arisen again and again, such as forgiveness, anger, deconstruction and the place of our bodies in post-traumatic remaking. This book will be challenging to some readers as it will require critical engagement with their own beliefs and the Christian teachings they have absorbed. It will upend some received wisdom. It will ask you to explore ways of thinking differently about yourself, your relationship with God, and even the kind of God you believe in. Remaking yourself after trauma is hard.

The practices in this book are offered in the hope that some or all of them might support a process of post-traumatic remaking that draws you closer to God.

The practices

The term 'spiritual practices' conjures up all kinds of traditional ideas – fasting, days in silence, Benediction and Adoration, pilgrimage, prayer, to name but a few. A strict definition of the term is not necessarily helpful for this book, but it might be useful if we broadly centre a sense of what we are talking about when we use the term 'spiritual practice'. In a simple sense, this is any activity – frequent or infrequent – that enables the practitioner to find peace, make meaning, and connect with the divine. This is purposefully quite vague and not specifically Christian. This book is particularly aimed at those who identify as Christian, but I hope it might be helpful on a broader level to those with other kinds of spiritual lives and faith beliefs. From a Christian perspective, we might refine this definition further and talk of spiritual practices as activities that draw us closer into union with God, and in doing so enable our restoration and our meaning-making.

The practices I have selected to develop in this book are practices of:

- Unforgiveness
- Anger
- Hopelessness
- Deconstruction
- Protest
- Pleasure
- Eating good food
- Rest

All of these are themes that have appeared over the years in my research and writing and that I wanted the opportunity to explore further. For each theme, I have examined the topic via Scripture, theology, psychology and other interdisciplinary fields in order to understand biblical texts and Christian traditions in the light of contemporary developments in a range of fields. So, for example, in the chapter on unforgiveness, I unpick the idea that to harbour unforgiveness is bad for one's psyche, that it will rot you away from the inside. It turns out that psychology research tells us this is not true. So what, therefore, does Jesus' command to practise unlimited forgiveness mean for the trauma survivor?

For each of these practices, in addition to the theoretical exploration, I have suggested a form of embodied spiritual practice – a practice that specifically seeks to involve the body. As I will outline in the following chapter on post-traumatic remaking, paying attention to the body in these kinds of practices is essential. The trauma survivor cannot talk their way out of trauma (although talking therapies are very useful); there must be a retraining of and reconnection to the body in order for the self to realize and believe that the danger has passed. I have tried to pay real attention to how our bodies might engage in these practices. Some of the practices are easier than others in this regard. For example, a spiritual practice of eating good food has a fairly logical practice entailed within the theme itself. A practice of deconstruction is a little trickier! So please take these suggestions as just that – suggestions. If you have better ways of embodying the kind of remaking required in relation to each theme, then go for it (and then get in touch to let me know what they are).

What is radical about these practices?

I have termed these spiritual practices as 'radical' in the title of this book. But what, exactly, is radical about them? The word 'radical' stems from the Latin word *radix* meaning 'root'. Christians might be familiar with this Latin word as it is one that appears in Advent as one of 'The O Antiphons' each liturgical year: *O Radix Jesse*. *Radix* here means 'root' and is taken from Isaiah 11.10: 'On that day the root of Jesse shall stand as a signal to the peoples; the nations shall inquire of him, and his dwelling shall be glorious.' Jesse is the father of King David in the Hebrew Bible. The 'root of Jesse' is an allusion to the coming of Christ (hence its inclusion in Advent liturgies) – the one promised from the House of David. The word 'radical' then takes its reference from something that originates in the root or the ground. When applied to body parts or bodily fluids, radical means 'vital to life'. When applied to politics it usually refers to someone who is aiming for thoroughgoing reform – someone who thinks that the way in which things are currently being done is so wrong that the whole system needs to change from the *root* up.

In what sense, then, are the spiritual practices proposed in this book radical? I take, from the etymological exploration of the term 'radical' above, two central themes. One is the theme of a foundation from which beautiful, embodied, incarnate things grow. And the other is the sense of vitality to life. These practices are *radical* in that they offer a different kind of foundation from which beautiful, embodied and incarnate things can grow. That is not to say that there is anything wrong with more traditional forms of spiritual practice such as contemplative prayer, confession, worship, fasting, hospitality or *lectio divina*. Indeed, these are vital to life and good spiritual and life-giving things can grow from them. Rather, these *radical* practices are ones that are rooted in a foundation of taking the experience of trauma seriously, wrestling with the theological questions such trauma inculcates, and developing spiritual practices out of this wrestling. These radical practices recognize the essential nature of the embodied element to post-traumatic remaking. Just as O *Radix Jesse* refers not to abstract ideas but to the real, incarnate human Christ, so do these radical practices place our embodiedness front and centre. These radical spiritual practices are important companions to the practices we are more familiar with and, as I demonstrate throughout this book, are practices found (or rooted in those found) throughout the Christian tradition.

That these practices are vital to life is, I hope, profoundly obvious. The activity of post-traumatic remaking of the self is

INTRODUCTION

a life-focused task. It is centred on survival. The French root of this word 'survive' reveals much. *Vivre* means to live and *sur* means above or on top. To *sur-vivre*, then, can mean so much more than simply not dying. It speaks, instead, to a process of flourishing, of not being dragged down and drowned by the experience of trauma. Radical spiritual practices are life-giving ones, practices that speak to both the ongoing nature of the trauma experience and the survival of those who experience it. To say that the goal of post-traumatic remaking of the self is survival is not to minimize what is on offer to the trauma survivor but rather to understand that goal as *sur-vivre* – finding ways to live above the trauma experience, finding ways to flourish. To call these *radical* spiritual practices is, then, to see them as practices that offer new roots for new flourishing.

These radical practices are also ones that subvert, resist and challenge conventional Western attempts to police and discipline certain types of affect and certain types of bodies. Particularly as we seek out ways to articulate the kinds of spiritual practice that are genuinely required by trauma survivors, we will need to resist making other people comfortable with our emotional responses. Matthew Potts, in his radical revisioning of the concept of forgiveness, notes:

> Instead, with social norms looking over her shoulder, the forgiving victim must ask, Is my anger uncomfortable to others? Are my emotions the real sin? Am I obligated to abate my rage for the sake of my abuser's feelings? The collapse of anger abatement and reconciliation into a single, passive forgiveness shifts away from a question of how a victim should respond to real harm and instead invites the regulation of the victim's emotional state.[1]

We will take, in this book, the radical step of strongly rejecting any invitation or expectation that survivors of trauma should regulate their emotional state for the sake of the comfort of others. Recognizing that this urge to disciple affect and emotion is inherently linked in Western thought to the disciplining of certain types of bodies, these radical practices will resist such disciplining and make space for bodies to exceed their (polite) boundaries.

How to use this book

You can use this book in a couple of different ways. If you want to, you can read it from start to finish, pausing to experiment with the different spiritual practices you encounter that you feel might be helpful for you. I encourage you to try them all if you can. Sometimes we trauma survivors are not very good (for a whole variety of complex reasons) at recognizing what is missing or lacking for us, and therefore we might not always recognize what helpful spiritual practices look like. We might not know something is going to be useful until we give it a go. Keeping a journal of your spiritual experiments might also be helpful in gauging when you are ready to move on from a particular practice.

On the other hand, you might want to dip into a particular chapter to start with that you can recognize straight away will be something you want to try. You might, for example, know that you are angry and be looking for a spiritual practice that utilizes this anger. This book does not have to be read in a linear way, starting at the beginning and finishing at the end. It can be dipped into as you want. Again, keeping a journal or using some of the margins and blank space in this book to keep notes about your practice might be helpful.

The process of post-traumatic remaking of the self is, as I will explore in the next chapter, rarely linear. It is not a series of progressive stages where you can begin with A and end with Z. It is less like a 100-metre race and more like a pilgrimage without a map. It is an ongoing, iterative, often lifelong process in which some familiar landmarks and quagmires will be passed by and sunk into repeatedly. This is normal. I often liken the work of post-traumatic remaking of the self to the alcoholic who, in their sixties might still refer to themselves as an alcoholic, even if they have not touched a drop of alcohol since their twenties. The work of staying sober is never completed; but

INTRODUCTION

rather, it is a daily choice. For many survivors of trauma, the work of remaking is not a task with a finish line, but rather a lifelong journey, an ongoing pilgrimage. You might, therefore, dip into this book on many occasions. It might sit on your shelf for years at a time until you need to engage with some or all of these practices again. It might be a constant companion; an ongoing reminder that God remains with you.

Notes

1 Matthew Ichihashi Potts, *Forgiveness: An Alternative Account* (New Haven, CT: Yale University Press, 2023), p. 144.

I

The Post-Traumatic Remaking of the Self

What happens after trauma? What is required of the trauma survivor when the experience of trauma is over if they want to try to move forward? The term I give to this activity is 'post-traumatic remaking of the self', rather than using terms like 'healing' or 'recovery'. Both of these two terms are, I think, insufficient descriptors of the complex and sustained nature of the work required by the trauma survivor in the aftermath of a trauma experience. The term 'recovery' implies a going-backward movement; a return to a pre-traumatized state. This is not what happens in the aftermath of trauma. There is no return to who one was before the trauma. This realization can be very distressing for trauma survivors and, indeed, for their loved ones. Similarly, I do not use the term 'healing' to describe the work that trauma survivors engage with in the aftermath of trauma. The word 'healing' comes with a whole heap of Christian baggage. This term can imply, particularly in the context of Christian language, a wiping out of the trauma experience, being 'cured' from the impact of trauma by God. Again, this is language that does not do justice to the experience of trauma survivors. Using language of healing can also set up unhelpful expectations in terms of the activity of God in such experiences.

I prefer to use the term 'post-traumatic remaking of the self'. This term reflects the experience of trauma survivors who 'frequently remark that they are not the same people they were before they were traumatized'.[1] This term is a helpful one for a number of reasons. First, it places this activity in relation to the trauma experience. It is a *post*-traumatic activity, that is, not an activity that can be engaged with in the midst of a trauma experience. It has been well established in psychological work that this remaking activity requires a safe space, a place in which one is not vulnerable to more traumatic experiences[2] – as best one can determine, anyway. No one is ever really invulnerable to trauma.

Second, the activity of post-traumatic remaking of the self is a *remaking* activity. Emphasizing the remaking nature of the task ahead of the trauma survivor implies that, in the experience of trauma, something is broken apart, damaged, or ruptured. The term 'rupture' is a common term in trauma literature and has its roots in the Latin word *ruptūra* meaning to break or to burst. This word, in Latin, is usually applied to the breaking or bursting of something bodily, such as skin or a vein. This is particularly interesting when we consider the essential place of the body in the practice of post-traumatic remaking of the self.

Third, the activity of post-traumatic remaking of the self is a *self*-focused activity. The implication here is that the experience of trauma causes damage to the self. While this is a term we use frequently in contemporary life (self-esteem, self-care, self-service, self-inflicted, etc.), it is worth taking a moment to understand exactly what we are referring to in the use of this word. From a philosophical perspective, there is no single, settled account of what the 'self' is. Most philosophers would position the self as the centre of autonomous agency. This means it is the self that is responsible for actions and decisions and thus can be worthy of praise or blame for whatever is experienced. It is easy to see the ways in which trauma might undermine an account of the self as autonomous. Other philosophers understand the self as something embodied, drawing a strong connection between body and mind. This relationship is a complex one. We might lean into a distinctly materialist understanding of the self in which an indissoluble connection is drawn between body and mind and the self cannot be separated from the body. Again, given the ways in which the body can feel alien and out of control to the trauma survivor, it is easy to see how this way of thinking about the self might be undermined by the experience of trauma.

From a neurological and psychological perspective, the connection between trauma and damage to the self is abundantly clear. Research on neuroimaging of traumatized people revealed that there was almost no activation of the self-sensing areas of the brain.[3] This was a marked difference from non-traumatized people. 'What is your brain doing when you have nothing in particular on your mind? It turns out you pay attention to yourself: The default state activates the brain areas that work together to create your sense of "self".'[4] Much of the neurological research indicates that the parts of the brain responsible for sensory information are compromised through trauma, and that things like the limbic system in our bodies are hyperactivated. All of this compromises our sense of who we are and what we feel. Without these sensory inputs, what is the 'self'?

What does post-traumatic remaking of the self look like? There is no simple answer to this and the process of remaking will be specific to each individual survivor of trauma. However, these differing remakings will share some things in common. They will be embodied in some form or another. The trauma psychologist Bessel van der Kolk (if you haven't read his book *The Body Keeps the Score* then put this book down and go and buy it now!) reminds us that talking therapies (counselling, psychotherapy, psychiatry) will only take the trauma survivor so far. For the remaking of the self, an embodied element is required. Kolk writes:

> [T]he act of telling the story [of the trauma] doesn't necessarily alter the automatic physical and hormonal responses of the bodies that remain hypervigilant, prepared to be assaulted or violated at any time. For real change to take place, the body needs to learn that the danger has passed and to live in the reality of the present.[5]

The practices outlined in this book are aimed at addressing the spiritual element of this process of post-traumatic remaking of the self. My hope is that trauma survivors would engage with these practices in addition to helpful forms of talking therapy where available, and alongside common embodied practices such as breathwork and yoga which have long been considered helpful for trauma survivors.

The remaking process

There is no helpful checklist of steps a trauma survivor can go through, ticking off each one and at the end being 'cured' of their trauma. The remaking trauma survivors engage with is far more complex, iterative and messy. It does not work as a linear process (where you do A and then B and then C and then you are done). And the likelihood is that this work of remaking will never be completed, not through any incompetence of the survivor but simply because it is possible that the trauma experience is so deeply rooted in the body that it is impossible to excise it completely. But while there is no simple step-by-step process that a survivor can move through, there are common features of remaking that are likely to be similar for each trauma survivor.

The first point to note is that the work of remaking the self can only happen when the self is no longer experiencing the trauma event. This work begins when the trauma survivor is no longer in a place of vulnerability to that particular trauma: they are out of the domestic setting where abuse has occurred; they have left the spiritually abusive church; they have found safety away from the war. Of course, as humans we are never invulnerable to all dangers. The point here is that the particular experience that caused us trauma is no longer physically present in our lives, even if it continues to be present in our bodies. A place of safety, of sanctuary, is necessary for the survivor to recognize that the physical impact of trauma that has caused the hyperarousal in their body is no longer necessary and begin to do the work of dialling down that perfectly understandable trauma response.

Attending to your body is another key feature of this post-traumatic remaking of the self. Remembering that the self is an embodied being – there is no self apart from your body – means that there is an embodied element to this post-traumatic remaking. Processing narrative and engaging in the abstract work of meaning-making is, as we shall see next, important, but this work is only useful, restorative and promoting of flourishing when it is undertaken in conjunction with attention to the body. Bessel van der Kolk notes:

> The body keeps the score. If the memory of trauma is encoded in the viscera, in heartbreaking and gut-wrenching emotions, in autoimmune disorders and skeletal/muscular problems, and if mind/brain/visceral communication is the royal road to emotion regulation, this demands a radical shift in our therapeutic assumptions.[6]

The body keeps the score. Kolk's research makes it abundantly evident that trauma is held in the body, so that the language we use like 'heartbreaking' or 'gut-wrenching' is not *merely* metaphor but often quite literal descriptions of what emotional trauma responses feel like. Trauma is held in the deep, non-rational part of the brain. It cannot be reasoned with or rationalized. Attending to the body is, therefore, an essential part of this remaking activity.

While attending to our bodies in the activity of post-traumatic remaking of the self is essential, that is not to say that verbal, reasoning, and rational activities are not also significant. To turn to Kolk again, I note that he does not suggest doing away with talking therapies altogether; indeed, he himself continues to practise as a psychiatrist (albeit one who pays deliberate attention to the embodied nature of trauma throughout his work). The process of constructing a narrative about the experience of trauma that allows meaning-making and promotes flourishing is also an essential part of this remaking. Given the fragmentary nature of trauma memory and the ways in which the brain often blocks, for the survivor's safety, the specific memories of the trauma experience, this narrative construction is often an iterative, piecemeal form of storytelling. It may need to be revisited many times over as new memories or new ways of telling the narrative emerge. But two things are significant when it comes to this narrative construction. First, it is essential that this narrative is not simply a reliving, a re-enactment of the trauma experience. A symptom of trauma is the way in which the past trauma event often tries to break through into the present through flashbacks, nightmares and hallucinations in which the trauma survivor does not merely remember the trauma but physically experiences the trauma again. Re-enacting trauma experience through narrative is not the goal here. Rather, it is a way of framing the trauma experience so that the trauma survivor is able to *sur-vivre* – to rise above, to not be drowned by the experience any longer.

The third significant element in the construction of the trauma narrative is that this narrative needs to be witnessed. It needs to be heard and to be believed by another. The witnesser – the observing, non-judgemental listener – is part of the creation of the knowledge held in the trauma narrative. Their very presence enables the co-creation of the narrative. Dori Laub – a Holocaust survivor, psychiatrist and psychotherapist – notes that:

> [T]he victim's narrative – the very process of bearing witness to massive trauma – does indeed begin with someone who testifies to an absence, to an event that has not yet come into existence, in spite of the overwhelming and compelling nature of the reality of its occurrence.[7]

It is through telling the narrative of the trauma experience to a witness that the trauma comes into existence, even as it has already been making itself known in the body. The very act of telling the narrative to a witness testifies to the reality of the experience and, therefore, the legitimacy of the ways in which a trauma survivor has been feeling. As many people with neurodivergence or people with chronic illnesses often note, although a diagnosis of a condition does not necessarily bring with it a cure, the very fact that this *thing*, this *way of being*, has a name and is not irrational can be a great relief and often very liberating.

There is one final element to add to this cluster of characteristics of post-traumatic remaking of the self – final, that is, not because it happens last but simply because our language requires something to come at the end of a list. Alongside being in a place of safety, attending to the surviving body and constructing a narrative that is witnessed, this final element is the re-establishment of relationships or the reconnection with society. A symptom of trauma is often the isolation of the self, withdrawal from friends or social groups, a removal of the self from activities that have often brought joy before the trauma experience. As the process of remaking is undertaken, this usually brings with it a desire to not be on one's own quite so much. This might mean re-establishing connections from before the trauma, but it is also likely that there is no going back. For example, if the trauma experience is connected to spiritual abuse, then going back into the church where that occurred is not necessarily a helpful idea. But there might be a desire to seek out a new church community that would enable the survivor to flourish. Often this reconnection with society comes with a desire to make the trauma experienced a gift of sorts. That is to say that, for some trauma survivors, reconnection with society might be motivated by a desire to advocate for change so that no one else has to go through what you went through. Or it might be motivated by study, writing and speaking so that your experiences can be shared, your insights brought to light, and you help to equip others to care for those who are traumatized or prevent further traumas from happening. It is no coincidence that many of the people working in trauma theology today are writing out of their own experiences of trauma.

The spiritual dimension

But the spiritual dimension of the experience of trauma must not be overlooked. For those with Christian faith (and for many who would not necessarily consider themselves people of faith), such experiences raise profound and challenging questions: how could God let this happen to me? Where was God when X was happening? Why hasn't God punished X for what they did to me? If God has a plan for my life, why would it include X experience? These are very real questions that are rooted in the theology we learn, study and imbibe through sermons, songs, extemporary prayers, and all manner of Christian paraphernalia! The wall sign that says, 'I know the plans I have for you, says the Lord, plans to prosper you and not to harm you' or the mug that reads, 'I can do all things through Christ who strengthens me.' The danger of proof-versing (taking individual verses out of context to make a particular, usually positive, point) is well known and I do not need to rehearse it here. Suffice to say, when theological reflection is shallow and/or self-serving, that theology quickly lets us down when times get tough. The spiritual element in post-traumatic remaking of the self is not to find answers to the questions listed above, but rather to come to a place where we realize that these are not the right questions to be asking in the first place. Part of the remaking required in the aftermath of the trauma experience is, for the Christian, a remaking of theology.

The suggestion that, alongside the self, there is a theological remaking required in the aftermath of trauma offers up an intriguing connection between theology and the self. Theology, of course, influences and shapes the ways in which we understand the world around us, the events that take place both on the world stage and in the domestic, personal arena, our sense of time, and how we make meaning in our lives. Theology is, therefore, intimately connected to the self, especially if we take a more narrative approach to the self. John Locke, for example, identified the self with a set of continuous memories, an ongoing narrative of one's past that is extended with each new experience.[8] If this ongoing narrative of the self is shot through with shallow, prosperity-Gospel-esque, proof-texting theologies which have contributed to the ongoing narrative and meaning-making of one's life, then in the aftermath of trauma this theological-self will necessarily require remaking.

Alongside the danger of using proof-texts that promote a very shallow understanding of theology, more traditional academic forms of theological discourse have also been found wanting in the face of the experience of trauma. Some of things that have been taken for granted in theology are disrupted and upended by trauma. Since the beginning of the twenty-first century, there has been a marked increase in interest in trauma from theologians (among many other disciplines), and various theologians have engaged in work that attempts to reimagine theology that does better justice to the experience of surviving trauma. This has often involved taking on particular doctrines and drawing them into dialogue with the embodied experience of trauma. It is worth remembering here (as I regularly remind my students) that all theology is human-made. It does not drop down from heaven in a complete orthodox form. The (human written) Creeds give shape to principles of orthodoxy but the specific workings out of theological doctrine are done by fallible, biased humans who only have very particular experiences of the world. And of course, for most of the history of theology, the humans who wrote (influential) theological texts existed in places of privilege, usually as educated, European/North Atlantic-centric, able-bodied, straight(ish), white men. For much of history, theology was written by a group of humans who were statistically less likely to experience trauma! It is no wonder that elements of theological discourse need remaking alongside the self in the aftermath of trauma.

Holy Saturday

This book is a book for those of us who live in Holy Saturday. While I will explore the theme of Holy Saturday in much more detail in the later chapter on rest, it is worth noting that one of the most significant themes in trauma theology has been that of Holy Saturday, developed and explored by Shelly Rambo in her book *Spirit and Trauma: A Theology of Remaining*. In this book, Rambo points to the ways in which Christians tend to rush to the happy ending. She pins this down specifically in terms of the experience of Easter. Christians, Rambo argues, want to rush straight from the horror of the crucifixion of Jesus to the victory of the resurrection. But we forget that there is a whole day in between these two things. A day in which there is no hope of resurrection because the disciples of Jesus have not understood what Jesus has told them. Holy Saturday is a day of fear, of death, of grief, of sadness, of incomprehension. Holy Saturday is a day where the boundaries of death and life become blurry and fixed linear patterns of life fall apart. It is a day where God (Jesus) is dead and yet God (Spirit) remains.[9]

Trauma survivors live in Holy Saturday, at least for a while. The experience of trauma blurs the easy lines between death and life. It is a place where it is not possible to simply skip ahead to the happy ending of the resurrection and the victory of Jesus. That is not to say those things are not true. They are. But the trauma survivor cannot yet encounter these things in a meaningful way. Holy Saturday is therefore a space that is temporal (as in the day occurs each year), liturgical (there is space in the day of Holy Saturday to experiment with liturgies that might recognize the experience of the trauma survivor), and experiential (a trauma survivor might experience Holy Saturday for a period of time in their lives). The practices outlined in this book are Holy Saturday practices. They are practices for the time of despair, incomprehensibility, anger, fear and grief. They are practices that might sustain our relationship with the God Who Remains in the midst of Holy Saturday until such time (if at all) that we are ready to remember and live into the resurrection.

Appendix: Holy Saturday liturgies

As an appendix to this book, I am so pleased to include some liturgical resources for Holy Saturday. These were developed by some students of mine who are ordinands in the Church of England as part of an undergraduate course on Theology and Trauma. They offer some sample liturgies and some resources about themes and liturgical choices for Holy Saturday. The resources they produced were simply outstanding and I wanted to make them available to people as part of this book of spiritual practices for trauma survivors. While they are more formal resources in that they are focused on a liturgy to take place within a church on Holy Saturday, they offer a profound contribution to this work and I am delighted to make them available to you as well.

Notes

1 Susan J. Brison, *Aftermath: Violence and the Remaking of a Self* (Princeton, NJ: Princeton University Press, 2002), p. 38.

2 See, for example, chapter 8 on 'Safety' in Judith Herman, *Trauma and Recovery: The Aftermath of Violence – From Domestic Abuse to Political Terror*, 2nd edn (New York: Basic Books, 1997).

3 Robyn L. Bluhm et al., 'Alterations in Default Network Connectivity in Posttraumatic Stress Disorder Related to Early-Life Trauma', *Journal of Psychiatry & Neuroscience: JPN* 34, no. 3 (May 2009), pp. 187–94.

4 Bessel van der Kolk, *The Body Keeps the Score: Mind, Brain and Body in the Transformation of Trauma* (St Ives: Penguin, 2015), p. 90.

5 van der Kolk, *The Body Keeps the Score*, p. 21.

6 van der Kolk, *The Body Keeps the Score*, p. 86.

7 Dori Laub, 'Bearing Witness or the Vicissitudes of Listening' in *Testimony: Crisis of Witnessing in Literature, Psychoanalysis, and History*, ed. Shoshana Felman and Dori Laub (New York & London: Routledge, 1992), p. 57.

8 John Locke, *An Essay Concerning Human Understanding*, ed. A. D. Woozley (New York: New American Library, 1974), pp. 210–20.

9 Shelly Rambo, *Spirit and Trauma: A Theology of Remaining* (Louisville, KY: Westminster John Knox Press, 2010).

2

The Practice of Unforgiveness

> Then Peter came and said to him, 'Lord, if my brother or sister sins against me, how often should I forgive? As many as seven times?'
> Jesus said to him, 'Not seven times, but, I tell you, seventy-seven times.'
> (Matt. 18.21–22)

It seems both obvious and essential that the Christian forgive. After all, Jesus specifically instructs his followers, as in the parable of the Unmerciful Servant (quoted above), that there should be no limits on our forgiveness of those who sin against us. When Jesus teaches us how to pray, he includes the line 'forgive us our debts, as we also have forgiven our debtors' (Matt. 6.12). It's the thing that everyone knows about Christians – they are the ones who forgive. Christian history and literature abound with examples of those who forgive the terrible sins that are wrought against us, in ways that seem unbelievable. Modelling themselves after Jesus who, on the cross, prayed that those who committed these acts of violence to him would be forgiven by God, so do Christians often (seemingly unbelievably) forgive those who sin against them. Famously Gee Walker, after the racially motivated murder of her son Anthony Walker in 2005, said of those who murdered Anthony, 'I've got to forgive them. I still forgive them. My family and I still stand by what we believe: Forgiveness.'[1] Similarly, in the aftermath of the murder of nine members of the Emanuel African Methodist Episcopal Church in Charleston, South Carolina by white supremacist Dylan Roof, Nadine Collier, the daughter of Ethel Lane, one of Roof's victims, said, 'I forgive you.' She was not alone, as many (but not all) of those family members gathered at Roof's hearing offered similar statements of forgiveness. Forgiveness – it's what Christians do.

In addition to understanding forgiveness as something explicitly commanded by Jesus, we believe we know why we are supposed to forgive. Yes, it is the following of a divine commandment. But it is also good for us. Holding on to unforgiveness, so the popular wisdom goes, is bad for us spiritually, mentally, emotionally and physically. If we harbour unforgiveness we are only hurting ourselves. Unforgiveness festers inside us and rots us away like a fruit with a rotten core.

It is, therefore, quite common for Christians responding to trauma survivors to suggest that the trauma survivor needs to forgive the offender, the perpetrator of sins against them, before they are able to move on and flourish. It's not about how you feel, they insist, but rather is a choice we make every day. Jesus commands us to forgive, and to have no limits on that forgiveness. Therefore you must choose to forgive every day until, hopefully, one day that forgiveness 'sticks'.

This chapter upends this conventional wisdom and proposes a spiritual practice of unforgiveness. In doing so, I will unpick a number of assumptions that relate to forgiveness and unforgiveness from psychological and sociological perspectives. First, we will examine the assumption of a forgiveness/unforgiveness binary. Second, we will consider some of the contemporary research on unforgiveness and whether or not unforgiveness is only ever considered as something negative. Third, we will attempt to piece together a definition of 'unforgiveness' that is meaningful and accurate. Having done this, we can explore the impact contemporary research into unforgiveness in particular might have on biblical commands and directives towards forgiveness. As always, this is unsettling territory, but territory that I hope, nonetheless, will contribute towards practices that enable us to flourish.

The forgiveness/unforgiveness binary

Whenever I am teaching my students, I always say to them that if they are ever presented with a binary (black or white, male or female, body or soul, etc.) their 'binary antenna' should prick up because things are rarely ever as simple as an either/or choice between two things. Our binary antenna, therefore, should be on high alert when we see the choice of forgiveness or unforgiveness as a simple either/or binary. In the first instance, we should recognize that this is not a simple either/or choice; but we should then question whether or not unforgiveness is the opposite of forgiveness. Is it? I'm not so sure.

What is forgiveness? There has been an abundance of sociological and psychological research on the nature of forgiveness. In the 1950s, Fritz Heider described forgiving as the forgoing of vengeful behaviour. Heider believed this forgoing to be an expression of the victim's sense of self-worth.[2] Further research has characterized forgiveness as 'the reduction in avoidance motivation and revenge motivation following an interpersonal offence',[3] and has highlighted the idea that, when forgiving, a person 'experiences a transformation that causes him or her (a) to refrain from taking actions that might be perceived as protective of his or her self-interests but ultimately destructive for the relationship and, instead, (b) to engage in actions that contribute to relational health.'[4] In this research, unforgiveness is characterized as the very opposite of forgiveness. Early research also seemed to indicate that forgiveness and unforgiveness were controlled by the same processes and mechanisms, which further exemplified their oppositional nature.[5]

But this is not necessarily true. If it were, then the only way for unforgiveness to be reduced would be through forgiveness, and this is not the case. Unforgiveness can be reduced in a number of ways that do not include forgiveness, for example by seeking revenge, by restoring justice, or by obtaining counselling.[6] Unforgiveness and forgiveness are, therefore, distinct but interrelated constructs and 'the two are not necessarily reciprocals of each other'.[7] Forgiveness, therefore, is only one of many ways to reduce unforgiveness. But is reducing unforgiveness desirable or even necessary?

Unforgiveness is not always a bad thing!

It turns out that not forgiving someone might not actually be the travesty and self-destructive act we have assumed it to be. It can be, but it is not necessarily so. Unforgiveness is not a simple concept but can be highly nuanced. Early research suggested that unforgiveness was conceptualized as cold emotion and rumination[8] but this conceptualization lacks the nuance and variability with which unforgiveness is actually experienced. This affect-based view of unforgiveness has dominated theories around forgiveness and unforgiveness but doesn't take into account the cognitive and rational dimensions at play here. In other words, unforgiveness cannot be characterized as being simply a negative emotional state. Attention must be paid to the cognitive experiences of the unforgiver and we must avoid making assumptions about the nature of their emotions around unforgiveness. Suffice to say, unforgiveness is not always a bad thing!

There is plenty of research that suggests that, in some cases, unforgiveness is a positive and appropriate response. For example, Singh et al. note that, 'Unforgiveness is appropriate, justifiable, and morally legitimate in the face of some severe offenses, such as brutal murder, burglary, and sexual abuse ... and even for some minor transgressions.'[9]

There are some clearly documented benefits to unforgiveness as well. Unforgiveness has been shown to play a positive role in shaping friendships and interpersonal relationships.[10] It can enhance our abilities to adapt in the future in order to 'overcome negative situations, reduce burdens, acquire positive lessons, achieve greater satisfaction, and feel positive'.[11] Similarly, unforgiveness is positively linked to increases in self-worth, productivity and well-being and can be conceptualized as an appropriate form of self-care: 'Sometimes withholding forgiveness may enhance self-esteem and self-worth in victims, while granting forgiveness may cause emotional and psychological problems.'[12] Being unforgiving might also help to avoid future situations in which further transgression is likely to take place and encourage us to invest in more promising and productive relationships.

In the case of the trauma survivor, it is important to understand that trauma and forgiveness belong to two different worlds.[13] It turns out that forgiveness is not the primary way in which trauma is healed.[14] Alford notes that,

> The real work of coming to terms with the reality of the traumas we have suffered is so difficult and so painful, we turn to forgiveness in the hope that it will heal our pain and rage without having to go through the hard sorrow-filled work it takes to get there.[15]

As I noted in the introduction in respect of the work done in trauma theology around the place of Holy Saturday, often Christians are tempted to rush from the crucifixion to the resurrection – the happy ending – without recognizing the day of deep sorrow and despair that sits between them. Similarly, we can tout 'forgiveness' as the prescription for our negative experience of trauma without necessarily recognizing 'the hard sorrow-filled work' that is really required in the post-traumatic remaking of the self. Alford's research provocatively claims that in the case of trauma experiences 'forgiveness is often inappropriate. Forgiveness is frequently unnecessary for the work of life to go on.'[16] It *is* possible to move forward without forgiving and no longer be preoccupied with the offence or be weighed down with negative feelings of bitterness, anger and resentment about it.[17] If we only view unforgiveness as negative, we risk re-victimizing and re-traumatizing those unwilling or unable to forgive as somehow 'failing'.

The pressure to forgive people, the feeling that you ought to forgive and that you are not able to do so, can cause substantial distress.[18] This can be particularly compounded when the feeling that you ought to forgive someone is bound up with your faith. Not being able to do what Jesus commands us to do can lead to our perceiving our inability to forgive as something sinful, further contributing to distress.

A new way of thinking about unforgiveness

How do we begin to reconcile the (clear?) Christian teaching on forgiveness with the research from psychological and sociological disciplines that seem to suggest unforgiveness might, at times, be the most appropriate thing for our flourishing, especially in the aftermath of a trauma experience? We might reflect, as Christians, that forgiveness is embedded in the metanarrative of the Bible,[19] and indeed we might cite the kinds of teachings by Jesus that seem to prioritize acts of forgiveness. However, beyond these few references, there is actually very little in the New Testament about forgiveness! Paul mentions it only rarely. Matthew and Mark say less about forgiveness than Luke (who doesn't really say that much!), and the Johannine Gospel says nothing explicitly about forgiveness.[20]

A helpful step forward in thinking about unforgiveness is to recognize what forgiveness is and is not. Too often forgiveness becomes dependent, in some way, on reframing or overcoming our emotions. We alluded to this at the outset of this chapter in that forgiveness is often seen as a therapeutic tool. We are encouraged to forgive because the alternative, not forgiving, is bad for us. We can be tempted, notes Matthew Potts in his commentary on Jacques Derrida's work on forgiveness, 'to romanticize forgiveness, to regard it as an enchanted salve or unearned resolution'.[21] We need to resist this romantic vision of forgiveness. Forgiveness does not fix everything, the wrongs committed remain to be fixed even after any forgiveness has been offered. Many definitions of forgiveness are tied up with this idea that forgiveness entails some kind of overcoming or sublimation of emotions; that its grounds are basically affective ones.[22] To forgive, one might argue, is to ignore or squash feelings of anger, sadness, despair or rage, either for our own good (as a kind of therapeutic concern) or for the good of others (with regard to other people's comfort with our emotional states).

THE PRACTICE OF UNFORGIVENESS

We should also recognize, as we began to outline earlier, that forgiveness and unforgiveness do not exist on a spectrum. They are not in opposition to each other as some form of dyadic binary. The opposite of forgiveness might be better characterized as retaliation. This would mean that forgiveness could be understood as 'the commitment to forgo retaliation.'[23] With this in mind, I wonder if it might be possible to be willing to forgo retaliation while also resisting any specific forms of forgiveness, especially when the offending person is not repentant. Potts again notes, in his critique of Martha Nussbaum's philosophy of forgiveness:

> It seems to me both rationally and morally unnecessary that we ask victims to 'surrender feelings' of anger at injustice, feelings that through their witness might 'survive as a testimony and living memorial' for the sake of a philosophy of forgiveness that sits uncomfortably with anger.[24]

In the case of trauma, much of the traditional (Christian) teaching on forgiveness is insufficient and takes too little regard of the specificities of trauma and physiological capabilities of the trauma survivor. A case in point is the place of memory in forgiveness. What is required in forgiveness is a delicate balance of remembering well. This entails enough memory that the significance of the event for our own identity and meaning-making is recalled and understood, alongside enough forgetting that the memory of the event does not threaten to overwhelm us. What a delicate balance indeed! Especially for the trauma survivor who often will have no control with regard to when the ways in which the memory of the trauma event haunts them in their waking or sleeping. Similarly, many trauma survivors struggle to piece together specific memories of trauma events, such that the details of the trauma may continue to escape their grasp. What place memory here? Potts notes that:

> Restored relationship isn't constitutive of forgiveness, but the issue of healing is crucial. If forgiveness is about addressing past wrong, then it must engage discussions of traumatic

memory, of how our traumatic pasts persist into our presents, and the degree and manner by which those traumas can or should be managed or expunged.[25]

A spiritual practice of mourning

It might seem a little odd that, in a chapter on unforgiveness, I propose a spiritual practice of mourning as the practice connected to being unforgiving. Here I am indebted to the work of Matthew Potts who proposes that forgiveness 'is a self-reflexive and nonretaliatory ethical posture that begins and ends in failure, that it is a practice of mourning that reckons rather than redeems past wrong'.[26] I am sure Potts is right, but I also want to commend a practice of mourning as the way to engage with and embrace unforgiveness.

This practice of mourning commits us to accepting the incomprehension of our trauma. There is no neat resolution, no rationalization, no way of understanding the *why* of what we have experienced. Trauma is, after all, stored in the non-rational, non-cognitive parts of our brain that cannot be reasoned or discussed into wellness. So our practice of mourning recognizes that nothing can be done to repair the past or even to provide adequate redress in the present. In the face of this impossibility of compensation and of understanding, we refuse to have our emotions policed. Our righteous anger does not need to go anywhere. But it does need space for expression.

The practice of mourning I offer here has its grounds in the beautiful practice of *shiva* which our Jewish siblings engage in after the death of a close relative. Ever mindful of the risk of appropriating something that does not belong to the Christian tradition, I respectfully recognize the great psychological and spiritual value of the practice of *shiva* while recognizing that I cannot fully comprehend that which is not mine to experience.[27] In the vein of that respect, I offer a practice that is modelled after *shiva* without being an appropriation of it.

In the book of Job, after repeated attacks on Job by Satan that result in the loss of his family and property, and the infliction of ill health on Job, three of Job's friends who had heard of what happened to Job came to him to console and comfort him: 'They sat with him on the ground for seven days and seven nights, and no one spoke a word to him, for they saw that his suffering was very great' (Job 2.13). Here we find a mourning. Job tears his clothes and expresses his sorrow before God. His friends – who are worried about him – come to visit him at home in order to offer comfort and to console him. It is striking to me that the way they do this is by sitting with him in silence for a week.

Here is our practice of mourning. Set aside some time to mourn. This might be an evening or a day or a week. It might be once or it might be repeated. Invite a friend to come and mourn with you – one who you know can sit in silence and resist the urge to speak simply to feel more comfortable. This person will be a witness to your mourning, your unforgiveness and your trauma. Cover the mirrors in your home for this period of time. This will enable you to focus your energy on the work of mourning rather than on yourself and your 'presentability' in public places.

Express your anger and your unforgiveness. You might want to write or draw this instead of speaking it. You might want to take time to shout and scream and cry. Say out loud all the things good Christians are not supposed to say. Why me? Where were you, God, when this was happening to me? I hate you. You ruined my life. Fuck you.

When you have exhausted yourself, allow your friend to hold you and comfort you in silence. No words need to be spoken here. Your friend has witnessed your emotions and in hearing them has acknowledged that they are valid.

Wash your hands and your face. Feel the cooling water on your skin, the perfect antidote to the heat of rage and the puffiness of tears. Drink the cool water to soothe your throat. This is the gift of the Spirit that Jesus foretells in the Gospel according to John when he says, 'Let anyone who is thirsty come to me, and let the one who believes in me drink. As the scripture has said, "Out of the believer's heart shall flow rivers of living water"' (John 7.37b–38).

Light a candle. Just one. We are not into the full light yet, but as you light the candle, remember that even in the darkest of times, even in the deepest of Holy Saturdays, God remains. A small flicker of light is still light.

Eat together. Order a takeaway or eat your favourite food. Eat sweet things together. Enjoy rich tastes. Eat and take whatever pleasure you can in eating. As we eat, we signify our intention to go on living. We fuel our body for a little bit longer. We resist defeat even as we are not yet ready to proclaim victory.

Finally, pray. You do not have to think of any clever words or say anything you do not yet mean. You do not have to pretend to be in a different spiritual place from where you are. You do not have to engage in any dialogue with God if you are not yet ready to do so. You might know what you want to pray but, if not, I suggest you simply join with the angels' prayer – a prayer that is always true.

> Holy, holy, holy, the Lord God the Almighty, who was and is and is to come … You are worthy, our Lord and God, to receive glory and honour and power, for you created all things, and by your will they existed and were created. (Rev. 4.8, 11)

When/if you're ready to move forward

It is important to note that you may never get to this section of the chapter. You might need to spend the rest of your life in a place of mourning for what has been taken from you and for the forgiveness you have no capacity to offer. And this is OK. There is no right way to deal with a trauma experience.

However, one day you might be ready to take a step in turning this mourning into forgiving. You do not need to stop feeling angry. Righteous anger over what has been done to you is not a sin and forgiveness is not affective; forgiveness is not dependent on your emotions. Committing yourself to incomprehension, both of the trauma you experienced and of the overflowing, abundant grace and love of God, is essential. There is no repair of the past or possibility of redress in the present – you have been mourning this. To forgive is to lift your gaze towards the future and to recognize that forgiveness is finding a balance between memory and forgetting that allows place for the divine gift of doing as God does.

Notes

1 Evangelical Alliance, 'Mrs Walker Has Drawn on Her Christian Faith to Find Forgiveness for the Two Young Men Who Murdered Her Son Anthony', *Evangelical Alliance*, 1 December 2005, http://www.eauk.org/current-affairs/news/mrs-walker-has-drawn-on-her-christian-faith-to-find-forgiveness-for-the-two-young-men-who-murdered-her-son-anthony.cfm, accessed 28.06.2024.
2 Fritz Heider, *The Psychology of Interpersonal Relations* (Eastford, CT: Martino Fine Books, 2015).
3 Michael E. McCullough et al., 'Interpersonal Forgiving in Close Relationships: II Theoretical Elaboration and Measurement', *Journal of Personality and Social Psychology* 75, no. 6 (December 1998), p. 1587.
4 McCullough et al., 'Interpersonal Forgiving in Close Relationships', p. 1587.
5 Ajit Kumar Singh, Gyanesh Kumar Tiwari and Pramod Kumar Rai, 'Beyond "Cold Emotion and Rumination"', *European Journal of Psychology Open* 81, no. 2 (October 2022), p. 57.
6 Rachel W. Jones Ross, Susan D. Boon and Madelynn R. D. Stackhouse, 'Redefining Unforgiveness: Exploring Victims' Experiences in the Wake of Unforgiven Interpersonal Transgressions', *Deviant Behavior* 39, no. 8 (3 August 2018), p. 1070.
7 McCullough et al., 'Interpersonal Forgiving in Close Relationships', *Journal of Personality and Social Psychology* 73, no. 2 (1997), pp. 321–36.
8 Everett L. Worthington and Nathaniel G. Wade, 'The Psychology of Unforgiveness and Forgiveness and Implications for Clinical Practice', *Journal of Social and Clinical Psychology* 18, no. 4 (Winter 1999), p. 386.
9 Singh, Tiwari and Rai, 'Beyond "Cold Emotion and Rumination"', p. 58.
10 Susan D. Boon et al., 'Between Friends: Forgiveness, Unforgiveness, and Wrongdoing in Same-Sex Friendships', *Journal of Social and Personal Relationships* 39, no. 6 (1 June 2022), pp. 1693–716.
11 Singh, Tiwari and Rai, 'Beyond "Cold Emotion and Rumination"', p. 63.

12 Singh, Tiwari and Rai, 'Beyond "Cold Emotion and Rumination"', p. 68.

13 C. Fred Alford, *Trauma and Forgiveness: Consequences and Communities* (New York: Cambridge University Press, 2014), p. 1.

14 Alford, *Trauma and Forgiveness*, p. 10.

15 Alford, *Trauma and Forgiveness*, p. 1.

16 Alford, *Trauma and Forgiveness*, p. 1.

17 Jones Ross, Boon and Stackhouse, 'Redefining Unforgiveness', p. 1078.

18 Jones Ross, Boon and Stackhouse, 'Redefining Unforgiveness', p. 1076.

19 Anthony Bash, *Forgiveness and Christian Ethics*, New Studies in Christian Ethics (Cambridge: Cambridge University Press, 2007), p. 79.

20 Bash, *Forgiveness and Christian Ethics*, pp. 79–80.

21 Matthew Ichihashi Potts, *Forgiveness: An Alternative Account* (New Haven, CT: Yale University Press, 2023), p.55.

22 Potts, *Forgiveness*, p. 184.

23 Potts, *Forgiveness*, p. 21.

24 Potts, *Forgiveness*, p. 132 citing Margaret Urban Walker, *Moral Repair: Reconstructing Moral Relations after Wrongdoing* (New York: Cambridge University Press, 2006), p. 158.

25 Potts, *Forgiveness*, p. 183.

26 Potts, *Forgiveness*, p. 180.

27 For a full account of Jewish practices of death and dying see Simeon Schreiber, *From Mourning to Morning: A Comprehensive Guide to Mourning, Grieving, and Bereavement* (Jerusalem: Urim Publications, 2018).

3

The Practice of Anger

> Be angry but do not sin; do not let the sun go down on your anger. (Eph. 4.26)

Most Christians are probably familiar with the story in the Gospel of Matthew where Jesus enters the Temple in Jerusalem. In the Temple courts, Jesus finds money-changers, people selling and buying, and people selling doves for sacrifice in the Temple. He is angry and drives these people out of the Temple courts and overturns their tables. He says to them 'My house shall be called a house of prayer; but you are making it a den of robbers' (Matt. 21.13). Jesus gets angry and acts on this anger. He expresses what generations of Christians have referred to as 'righteous anger'. It is OK that Jesus gets angry in this instance, we say, because his anger is righteous. But I wonder if it is that simple? In this chapter I want to examine a traditional perspective on anger – that it is counter-productive and destructive – before turning our attention to the productive power of anger via thinkers such as Audre Lorde and Vincent Lloyd. Having explored these perspectives on anger, we will consider the aptness of anger in response to trauma experiences. This will enable us to contemplate a spiritual practice of anger – an angry rosary!

Anger only makes things worse

The American philosopher Martha Nussbaum famously articulated in her book *Anger and Forgiveness: Resentment, Generosity, Justice*[1] an Aristotelian account of anger as counter-productive. Nussbaum suggests that anger should be avoided even in circumstances of political injustice because of its tendency to alienate would-be allies, aggravate conflict and ultimately undermine the pursuit of just outcomes. Nussbaum argues that anger includes necessarily a desire to make the offending party suffer. In this approach, anger is never *apt* (we will return to this idea of the aptness of anger shortly) because it involves the false belief that revenge will undo the original harm. This anger is not rational, it's not a product of calm reasoning and therefore it is suspect and clearly *inapt*. In such philosophical accounts, anger marks a deviation from a well-ordered world.[2] Such a perspective on anger is named 'the counterproductivity critique'. This critique of anger argues that, quite simply, anger is counterproductive. In this critique, anger is something that burns hot and destroys things, relationships, and ultimately people (including the person who is angry). Therefore, we are told not to get angry because it only makes things worse.

Take, for example, the testimony of Christine Blasey Ford before the Supreme Court nominations committee. Blasey Ford testified to her sexual assault many years prior by the Supreme Court nominee Brett Kavanaugh. Because women are so often not believed, especially if they are angry, Blasey Ford had to ensure that every element of her communication was calm and free from any hint of anger. If she seemed angry, she would undo all the potential good her testimony was doing. Contrast Blasey Ford's calm and temperate demeanour with that of Kavanaugh himself who raged and whined throughout the testimony and resulting cross-examination.

The productive power of anger

Is anger really counterproductive? And is it counterproductive for everyone? The example of Blasey Ford and Kavanaugh might indicate that anger is really only counterproductive for some people. In fact, it might be important to note that getting angry is a particularly risky endeavour for women, especially for women of colour.[3] But I want to counter Nussbaum's assertions further still. Nussbaum's arguments that anger is always counterproductive and that it necessarily involves a revenge element seem to me to be demonstrably untrue. There are a number of ways in which we can consider anger to be productive.

The idiom 'Don't get angry, it only makes things worse' treats the counterproductivity of anger as a fixed fact rather than as a largely contingent feature of social reality.[4] It is, perhaps, therefore helpful to understand the counterproductivity argument as one that is an attempt at social control rather than any kind of manifestation of genuine concern for the angry or angry-tempted person. While there may be pragmatic and moral reasons for not getting angry – a moral duty to care for oneself, for example – we cannot argue that anger is *de facto* counterproductive.

In 1981 Audre Lorde – Black poet, activist and academic – delivered the keynote speech at the annual conference of the National Women's Studies Association. This speech was later published as an essay: 'The Uses of Anger: Women Responding to Racism'.[5] In this speech, Lorde highlights the fact that anger is a product of racism and that we must begin struggles for racial justice by acknowledging the anger it produces. It is this anger, Lorde argues, that must be harnessed as a tool. This anger can be transformed into action. She writes: 'Every woman has a well-stocked arsenal of anger potentially useful against those oppressions, personal and institutional, which brought that anger into being.'[6]

Lorde goes on to highlight specific ways in which anger can prove useful. She is writing in the context of the struggle for racial justice and therefore we must be careful to read her work in the context for which she intends it before broadening her work to consider how it might speak to the uses of anger more generally. What I mean to say is that if we are to read Lorde's work authentically, we should get angry about racism, as Lorde encourages us to do.

Lorde argues that anger can be a powerful source of energy that serves progress and change. When people allow their anger to fuel their action, things change. Anger produces discontentment with the status quo and a refusal to settle for anything less than an ideal world. Anger is how progress is made. Anger is loaded with information and energy.[7] It is good and productive, therefore, to get angry. This is how things change. Lorde writes, 'Anger expressed and translated into action in the service of our vision and our future is a liberating and strengthening act of clarification.'[8]

Lorde notes that she has used anger 'for illumination, laughter, protection, fire in places where there was no light, no food, no sisters, no quarter'.[9] Here it is the energy of anger that shines a light on areas of injustice. It is anger that nourishes when little nourishment can be found. It is anger that warms in the harsh cold of systemic oppression, in the arctic tundra of disbelief. It is anger that keeps us safe, preventing us from blindly walking back into dangerous situations where justice has not yet been found and modes of action have not yet changed. Sara Ahmed writes, 'Anger is creative; it works to create a language with which to respond to that which one is against, whereby "the what" is renamed, and brought into a feminist world.'[10]

It would seem obvious, then, that Nussbaum's claim that anger is counterproductive and, at best, a weapon of self-harm is false, or at least only partially true. Anger produces change, it reveals injustice, motivates action, sustains and nourishes, and can be creative. All of these things can be considered productive rather than counterproductive. We might even, alongside Vincent Lloyd, consider anger to be a theological rather than a secular thing:

> When we turn to marginalized voices, we find anger that embraces a theological rather than a secular idiom. We find anger marking an instance of domination rather than anger marking a moral wrong or social disorder. We find anger motivating interrogation of systems of domination rather than keeping us within the orbit of the normative order.[11]

Anger, in this instance, is prophetic. It highlights the inadequacies and insufficiencies of this world in relation to the ideal just world – the kingdom of God. Just as the prophets in the Hebrew Bible angrily demonstrate the ways in which the people of God have turned away from God's paths, so might our own anger motivate us to, in Lloyd's words, interrogate 'systems of domination' and reject the 'orbit of the normative order'. In other words, anger might allow us both to imagine and to participate in building a more just world, a world where the kingdom of God breaks in.

Resisting productivity

Does my anger *have* to be productive (rather than counterproductive) for it to be 'good'? While I think we can clearly argue that anger is not *by necessity* counterproductive, and thus might, at times, be productive, it is worth querying the link between productivity and goodness and the idea that framing anger as something productive might somehow redeem it. As Karen Bray argues:

> neoliberal economics relies on narratives in which not being in the right mode means a cursed existence. Its opening provocation is a diagnosis of a soteriological and theological impulse in neoliberalism that demands we be productive, efficient, happy, and flexible in order to be of worth and therefore get saved out of the wretched experience of having been marked as worthless.[12]

Resting on Max Weber's Protestant work ethic, Bray is peeling apart the relationship between economics, affect, productivity and salvation. While I do want to insist that anger is not *by necessity* counterproductive, I do not want to reinscribe the idea that anything, including our emotions, has to be productive in order to be righteous. I want to unlink in our minds the idea that productivity is a good judge of the value or worth of an affect, a person, a situation. I want to argue that un/productivity might be only one way in which we recognize the value of anger.

The aptness of anger

Amia Srinivasan picks up this resisting-productivity thread of anger in her work 'The Aptness of Anger'. Srinivasan asks, 'Is the anger, however unproductive, none the less *apt*?'[13] *Contra* Nussbaum who claims that anger is never apt, Srinivasan argues that anger is in response to a moral violation; a violation of not just how one wishes things were, but a violation of how things ought to be. Our anger, therefore, might be either productive or counterproductive, while still being apt; still being the most appropriate response to a situation or event. Apt anger can be counterproductive.

Srinivasan highlights what she terms 'affective injustice', which she defines as 'the injustice of having to negotiate between one's apt emotional response to the injustice of one's situation and one's desire to better one's situation – a conflict of responsibilities that are all but irreconcilable.'[14] The injustice is that one might have to moderate one's affective responses (that is, not appear angry) in order to better (or at least not worsen) one's situation. This is a psychic tax that is levied on victims of oppression.[15]

The anger of Jesus

In the Gospel of Matthew, Jesus prohibits anger. As part of the Sermon on the Mount, he tells his listeners, 'If you are angry with a brother or sister, you will be liable to judgement' (Matt. 5.22). However, as we have already read, Jesus himself is depicted as angry later in the same Gospel as he overturns the stalls in the Temple and chastises the merchants in the Temple courts. While the interpretation of this verse is not simple, for centuries Christians have relied on a distinction between virtuous and violent anger and between anger at a person and anger at their sin. Jesus, it is claimed by Augustine, was angry but not sinful. His rage was virtuous and righteous.[16]

This distinction between anger at sin rather than anger at people, and between virtuous and violent anger, is one that persisted through much of the medieval period. Theologians such as Gregory the Great and Bonaventure echoed Augustine's distinctions, always being clear that, while Jesus was angry, he did not, of course, sin. However, it is in the thinking of Thomas Aquinas that we find an extensive examination of the morality of anger and a rejection of the human/sin distinction. Aquinas argues that anger can be virtuous – we can see that in Jesus' anger in the Gospels – and that anger is not necessarily contrary to reason. Anger can be either reasonable or unreasonable (ST 2. II. Q.158). Anger that is aimed at the right person is reasonable. God only condemns anger that is not reasonable. Therefore, when Jesus prohibits anger in Matthew 5.22 we can infer that Jesus is not talking about all anger, but rather only a certain type of anger.

It is always useful to read verses from the Bible through their context. It is important to note, then, that this command regarding anger is given in the context of a prohibition against murder. In the preceding verse, Jesus is reminding his listeners that they have been commanded not to commit murder lest they face judgement. Jesus extends and intensifies this commandment by telling the listeners that not only should they not murder, they should not even get angry with a brother or sister. This condemnation of anger is clearly tied to the divine command not to kill. But even in this command, we know that the commandment is not totalizing. The possibility of execution via the death penalty was still permitted.[17]

How useful are these distinctions? Is it helpful for us to try to frame different types of anger (vicious/virtuous or directed towards humans/at sin) as binaries? I frequently tell my students that whenever they see a binary like this their 'binary antenna' should go up and put them on high alert. Things are rarely as simple as either/or and these binaries brush over complex middle spaces that are often well worth wrestling with.

I think it is fair to say that while we might want to emphasize virtuous anger at sin as the kind of anger that Jesus embodies in the Gospels, it is not always possible to make these kinds of distinction in the moment when anger erupts. This is not to say that anger is not rational – indeed, I think it often is – but rather to say that pausing at the moment of anger to engage in some philosophical and theological exploration is not helpful. Furthermore, is it even possible to be angry at sin and not angry at the person who committed the sin? Surely, as we understand people as whole psychosomatic beings, your actions and you are not so easily divisible. Like Aquinas, we can reject this human/sin distinction as offering an unhelpful distraction from more significant questions about anger.[18]

Anger for trauma survivors

It is often apt for a survivor of trauma to be angry and it is apt for them to be angry at both the sin of the person who caused their trauma and at the perpetrator themselves. Anger is a mode of post-traumatic remaking in which, like a prophet, the trauma survivor declares their discontent and rage at the state of the world that such a thing could happen to them. This anger is prophetic and creative. It participates in the building of a new world. We can understand anger, therefore, as a symptom of longing for the kingdom of God; it is the personification of the prayer 'thy will be done, on earth as it is in heaven.' Lloyd characterizes the discernment of anger as 'not theoretical work, but practical work; not individual work, but collaborative and coalitional work. To invoke another theological idiom, it is the work of conversion.'[19] The conversion here is in the breaking in of the kingdom of God; a remaking of the world with justice as its heartbeat. Anger is the prophetic cry of longing for how the world *should* be.

Anger as a spiritual practice

In this spiritual practice, I want to harness scriptural and theological resources as an outlet for prayer that does not require us to calm ourselves as a beginning point. It might be that contemplative states of prayer that are calming and peaceful are reached as a result of this practice but that is not, primarily, the goal of this work. The goal is to express anger and to allow it to be put to use, if you want to. Again, I make no assumption of the productivity or otherwise of anger. Your anger is likely apt. I think that is sufficient as a beginning place.

Let us pray an angry rosary. This can be done with any kind of rosary or set of prayer beads – whatever you have to hand and are most comfortable with. I suggest that you make this a collective act of prayer where possible, but it might be that you are not necessarily ready to do this immediately. Whenever you are ready. If you're not familiar with praying with beads, there are lots of good guides on the internet. I particularly like the guide on the Hallow website as a good starting point.[20]

Begin with the sign of the cross, praying as you hold the cross or starting bead in your hand.

In the name of God, Father, Son, and Holy Spirit. Amen.

Or if you would prefer a more gender-neutral invocation of the Trinity:

In the name of God, Creator, Redeemer, and Sustainer. Amen.

Move to the next bead – this is the invitatory bead. Here, as you hold this bead, pray the invitation:

- God make speed to save me.
- Lord make haste to help me.
- Glory to the Father, and to the Son, and to the Holy Spirit: as it was in the beginning, is now, and will be for ever. Amen.

If you have Anglican prayer beads, then, as you hold each bead in between your fingers, pray the Lord's Prayer (in any translation that works for you).

You could add in a psalm after each iteration of the Lord's Prayer or you could alternate between the Lord's Prayer and a psalm. There are plenty of suitable psalms – choose your favourite or mix it up. I suggest Psalm 28 as a good place to start:

To you, O Lord, I call; my rock, do not refuse to hear me,
for if you are silent to me, I shall be like those who go down to the Pit.
Hear the voice of my supplication, as I cry to you for help,
as I lift up my hands towards your most holy sanctuary.
Do not drag me away with the wicked, with those who are workers of evil,
who speak peace with their neighbours, while mischief is in their hearts.
Repay them according to their work, and according to the evil of their deeds;
repay them according to the work of their hands; render them their due reward.
Because they do not regard the works of the Lord, or the work of his hands,
he will break them down and build them up no more.
Blessed be the Lord, for he has heard the sound of my pleadings.
The Lord is my strength and my shield; in him my heart trusts;
so I am helped, and my heart exults, and with my song I give thanks to him.
The Lord is the strength of his people; he is the saving refuge of his anointed.
O save your people, and bless your heritage; be their shepherd, and carry them for ever.

If you are using traditional rosary beads, you can mix the traditional pattern of praying the rosary with some of our angry practices.

- The Sign of the Cross on the cross or crucifix.
- The Lord's Prayer at the first large bead (and each subsequent large bead).
- The Jesus Prayer on each of the three small beads. 'Lord Jesus Christ, Son of God, have mercy on me [a sinner].'[21]

You will then move into praying 'decades' (ten beads) as follows, repeating this cycle for each of the meditations outlined below:

- Announce the meditation ('The first meditation is…')
- The Lord's Prayer on the large bead.
- The Jesus Prayer on each of the ten small beads.
- In the gap between the last small bead and the next large bead pray this breath prayer:
    Inhale: 'Lord, let this anger burn brightly.'
    Exhale: 'Let it illuminate my path.'

Traditional praying of the rosary adds in the Mysteries of the Rosary which are meditations on episodes in the life and death of Jesus. Each decade is associated with a particular mystery that is kept in mind while praying. Here are five angry meditations from Scripture that you can meditate on through each decade of your rosary.

1. Jesus cleanses the Temple (Matt. 21.12–17).
2. Jonah gets angry with God (Jonah 4.1–6).
3. Job is angry with God (Job 3).
4. Paul is angry with the Galatians (Gal. 3).
5. Martha and Mary are angry with Jesus (John 11.17–36).

This outline is just a suggestion. If you have beads that lend themselves to a different pattern of prayer then feel free to innovate! There's no right way to do this. Just experiment, use the time to reflect, and find a rhythm of prayer that works for you.

When you're ready to move on

Like a fire, eventually your anger will begin to smoulder and fade. It cannot rage for ever. When you are ready to move on, consider ways in which your anger might be channelled into action. Or how you might participate in the building of God's kingdom on earth. You might switch out the angry breath prayers in the rosary for more peaceful ones:

- Inhale: God of all surpassing peace,
- Exhale: Comfort and protect me.

You might want to replace some of your angry prayers with more peaceful psalms, for example Psalm 121 or Psalm 4 (perhaps meditating on the final verse: 'I will both lie down and sleep in peace; for you alone, O Lord, make me lie down in safety.').

Notes

1 Martha Craven Nussbaum, *Anger and Forgiveness: Resentment, Generosity, Justice* (Oxford: Oxford University Press, 2016).
2 Vincent Lloyd, 'Anger: A Secularized Theological Concept', *Political Theology* 22, no. 7 (3 October 2021), p. 587, https://doi.org/10.1080/1462317X.2021.1986200.
3 Jilly Boyce Kay and Sarah Banet-Weiser, 'Feminist Anger and Feminist Respair', *Feminist Media Studies* 19, no. 4 (19 May 2019), p. 605.
4 Amia Srinivasan, 'The Aptness of Anger', *Journal of Political Philosophy* 26, no. 2 (2018), p. 133.
5 Audre Lorde, 'The Uses of Anger', *Women's Studies Quarterly* 25, no. 1/2 (1997), pp. 278–85.
6 Lorde, 'The Uses of Anger', p. 280.
7 Lorde, 'The Uses of Anger', p. 280.
8 Lorde, 'The Uses of Anger', p. 280.
9 Lorde, 'The Uses of Anger', p. 285.
10 Sara Ahmed, *The Cultural Politics of Emotion* (London: Routledge, 2013), p. 176.
11 Lloyd, 'Anger', p. 593.
12 Karen Bray, *Grave Attending: A Political Theology for the Unredeemed* (New York: Fordham University Press, 2020).
13 Srinivasan, 'The Aptness of Anger', p. 126.
14 Srinivasan, 'The Aptness of Anger', p. 134.
15 Srinivasan, 'The Aptness of Anger', p. 136.
16 William C. Mattison, 'Jesus' Prohibition of Anger (MT 5:22): The Person/Sin Distinction from Augustine to Aquinas', *Theological Studies* 68, no. 4 (1 December 2007), p. 843, https://doi.org/10.1177/004056390706800405.
17 Mattison, 'Jesus' Prohibition of Anger', p. 861.
18 Mattison, 'Jesus' Prohibition of Anger', p. 856.
19 Lloyd, 'Anger', p. 595.
20 Abby Fredrickson, 'How to Pray the Rosary: Guide to the Rosary Prayer', Hallow, 10 January 2023, https://hallow.com/blog/how-to-pray-the-rosary/, accessed 10.07.2024.
21 Note that ancient forms of the Jesus Prayer do not include the words 'a sinner' at the end. Feel free to pray this prayer in either form.

4

The Practice of Hopelessness[1]

'Hope is a fickle, dangerous thing. It steals your focus and aims it toward the possibilities instead of keeping it where it belongs – on the probabilities.'[2]

I have long had a complicated relationship with hope. For me, this stems from years in a charismatic evangelical church which proclaimed a 'hope in Jesus'. I was (and still am to some extent) perplexed about what this statement meant and why it was considered to be such a game-changer in evangelism and in discipleship. As I have explored some of the theologies of hope and the nature of hope, I have come to consider its significance in relation to its counterpart of hopelessness. In this chapter, I deconstruct the concept of hope and make a case for hopelessness as a spiritual practice that might be of use to the trauma survivor engaged in post-traumatic remaking.

Traditional Christian narratives of hope

In the Christian tradition, hope is most usually considered to be a theological virtue alongside faith and charity (or love). In the first letter to the Corinthians, Paul writes, 'And now faith, hope, and love remain, these three; and the greatest of these is love' (1 Cor. 13.13). This verse is couched in an eschatological context following on from Paul's famous declaration that, 'Now we see only a reflection, as in a mirror, but then we will see face to face. Now I know only in part; then I will know fully, even as I have been fully known' (1 Cor.13.12). The implication is that these theological virtues will also find their fullness in eternity. They are eschatologically oriented.

The eschatological orientation of hope is evident throughout the Scriptures. For example, in Ephesians 1.18 we find Paul praying that the hearts of the Ephesians would be enlightened by the Spirit so that they might know the hope to which they have been called, 'the riches of his glorious inheritance among the saints'. Similarly, in a section of Romans on 'future glory', we read, 'For in hope we were saved. Now hope that is seen is not hope, for who hopes for what one already sees? But if we hope for what we do not see, we wait for it with patience' (Rom. 8.24–25). Hope, here, is primarily hope in salvation, hope for eternal life.

For Aquinas, hope is similarly future-oriented. He defines natural hope as 'a future good, difficult but possible to attain ... by means of the Divine Assistance ... on whose help it leans' (ST II-II, 17.1). In this case, while hope is future-oriented, it is not solely eschatological. There is space within Aquinas' definition for the 'future good' that is hoped for to be attained, but only through the intervention of God. But of course, for Aquinas, hope is a theological virtue (as it was for Paul). In this sense:

> The theological virtue of hope (hope as a grace-infused habit of the mind) aims toward eternal happiness in God, and it enjoys divine assistance in obtaining that eternal happiness. In other words, the object of hope is God, and the means of obtaining the object is God's assistance ... the impossibly arduous goal of human perfection in God has become possible through Christ's suffering, death, and resurrection, and has been rendered attainable through the graced infusion of hope.[3]

Hope, in this perspective, is explicitly focused on eternal life, eternal happiness in God, and the state of perfection (in all things) that is to come in the eschaton. The virtue of hope is not present-oriented for Aquinas. Indeed, it is rooted in the triumph of the death and resurrection of Christ.

These themes are developed throughout Christian theology, nowhere more so than in the work of Jürgen Moltmann who wrote prolifically on hope in the middle of the twentieth century, shaping the theological discourse around hope for many decades. For Moltmann, the basis of the Christian hope rests in his characterization of God as one who suffers and, indeed, suffers with us. This God is a God who is moved and impacted by human suffering. Moltmann's theological accounts of hope are complex and shift throughout his lifetime, such that a brief description here cannot do justice to the breadth of his writings on the theme. But it is clear that, for Moltmann, the Christian hope is rooted in the cross. He writes:

> The cross of Christ is the sign of God's hope on earth for all those who lived here in the shadow of the cross. Theology of hope is at its hard core theology of the cross. The cross of Christ is the presently given form of the kingdom of God on earth. In the crucified Christ we view the future of God. Everything else is dreams, fantasies, and mere wish images. Hope born out of the cross of Christ distinguishes Christian faith from superstition as well as from disbelief. The freedom generated by the cross distinguishes Christian faith from optimism as well as from terrorism.[4]

While Moltmann does resolutely ground hope in the person of Christ and in his death and resurrection (interestingly moving away throughout his lifetime from the resurrection hope towards hope found in Christ's suffering and death), the hope here is one of promised relief from suffering in the new creation. Although he defends hope from superficial selfishness and otherworldly escapism,[5] this Moltmannian hope is resolutely eschatologically focused. This hope rests on divine solidarity and the divine eschatological promise of relief from suffering. But not in this life. Our hope is in the eternal life, not this one.

David Elliott, in his recent book *Hope and Christian Ethics*, offers a similarly eschatological perspective on hope. He writes, 'Theological hope ... provides an ultimate meaning and transcendent purpose to our lives; and it rejoices and refreshes us "on the way" (*in via*) with the prospect of ultimate reconciliation and lasting beatitude.'[6] Like Moltmann, Elliot's view of hope is rooted in an overarching metanarrative, a narrative in which lives have purpose and are on a journey towards union with God. Elliot's characterization of hope in this text is one that is 'supremely confident and triumphal'.[7] Theological hope has, according to Elliot, assured certainty as opposed to secular hope which is vain optimism. There is no room for doubt and uncertainty in Elliot's characterization of hope.

Boasting in our afflictions?

Before moving to consider the ways in which trauma experiences disrupt these characterizations of hope, I want to highlight one other biblical text on the theme. This text comes from Romans chapter 5. Indeed, any cursory search or scan of the book of Romans will find numerous references to hope within the text. But in chapter 5 the writer notes that

> we also boast in our afflictions, knowing that affliction produces endurance, and endurance produces character, and character produces hope, and hope does not put us to shame, because God's love has been poured into our hearts through the Holy Spirit that has been given to us. (Rom. 5.3–5)

This logic – affliction produces endurance produces character produces hope – is deeply engrained in the Christian psyche. It is often heard in testimonies. It is often the expected outcome of any difficulty experienced. It is a common way in which Christians try to make sense of, and indeed to justify, negative experiences in their lives, and often in the lives of others. Texts like this form a pedagogical connection between suffering and hope. If hope is a theological virtue, one to be cultivated and nurtured, then the experience of affliction is argued to be valuable in producing that virtue. The hope here that does not disappoint, however, is an eschatological hope. God's love and the assurance of perfect beatification in the new creation is the hope which does not disappoint.

The toxicity of hope

It is, of course, no surprise to discover that this kind of eschatological hope has been regularly criticized by theologies that take into account the vulnerable realities of people's lives. The promise of liberation, freedom from suffering, and joy in the new creation has been used to keep people in their place for centuries. Such logic was used, alongside narratives of providence, to keep slaves in slavery, to justify poverty, to prevent uprisings, and to maintain control. It was these kinds of Christian hope that prompted Karl Marx to write that, 'Religion is the sigh of the oppressed creature, the heart of the heartless world, and the soul of soulless conditions. It is the opium of the people.'[8] This kind of hope can be stultifying, drugging, paralysing; it can prevent the questioning of our context and experiences and lull us into obedience to systems and influences that should be challenged and uprooted.

Hope can be toxic and terrorizing. Hope is bound up with proof-texting verses such as Jeremiah 29.11 and Romans 8.28 where the implication is that one should have hope because God is in control of the things that happen in our lives. In the experience of trauma, the idea of God as one in control of all things and one who intervenes in our lives has already been destabilized.

The fact that these verses are often 'given'[9] to trauma survivors speaks to a second toxic aspect of hope – its imposition. Hope is often imposed on the trauma survivor by those around them. This is well meaning and often, I think, comes from a desire to hold hope for those whom people love. However, it can become toxic when such hope relies on a providential understanding of God that has no basis in reality. Such hope has no room for despair and hopelessness. This kind of hope is a privilege. It soothes the conscience of the one offering it but requires no action, imposes no ethical demand on that person. Such hope is possible when the privilege a person enjoys allows for the possibility of a future. In the experience of trauma, there is – in that moment, at least – no possibility of a future.

Optimism is not hope

In reality, this kind of hope is often optimism masquerading as hope. Optimism and hope are not the same thing. Optimism is a personality trait, a sense of approaching the world as generally providing positive outcomes for oneself and one's loved ones. Optimism can be good for your physical and mental health.[10] However, hope is not the same thing. Hope is an act of will – that virtue to be cultivated. Terry Eagleton comments on the difference between hope and optimism, noting that

> the most authentic kind of hope is whatever can be salvaged, stripped of guarantees, from a general dissolution. It represents an irreducible residue that refuses to give way, plucking its resilience from an openness to the possibility of unmitigated disaster. It is thus as remote from optimism as could be imagined.[11]

Of course, Eagleton is not talking about Christian hope here specifically but rather drawing a distinction between secular forms of hope and optimism. For Eagleton, hope is that which remains, that which is found when all else is stripped away. This hope recognizes reality and the potential for future disaster and disappointment and is yet able to remain even in the face of these things. Optimism is not like this. Optimism instead is a privilege – one borne out of the security of the present: 'Optimists are conservatives because their faith in a benign future is rooted in their trust in the essential soundness of the present.'[12] This trust in the essential soundness of the present is, in a Christian sense, what enables well-meaning people in church to impose 'hope' in such dangerous ways. Such trust in the essential soundness of the present rests, for these Christians, on a confidence in God's providential ways. A confidence that is, as we saw in the previous chapter, unfounded.

Hope, in this context, is triumphal. It is usually rooted in either the death of Jesus – and thus given meaning through the idea of Jesus' solidarity in suffering and significance through his ultimate resurrection from death – or solely in the resurrection of Jesus. In the second grounding, the death of Jesus is bypassed almost entirely except to the extent that this death makes the resurrection possible. While the hope offered might not be exclusively eschatological – that is, those who offer it are genuinely offering hope within this life and not only for the next – such hope is, inevitably, couched in eschatological terms. Resting on ideas of providence – God's hand at work in the paths of our lives – such hope has an end point in sight: God's providence leading us towards a happy ending in the new creation. I do not want to cast doubt on the eschatological vision of a place in which suffering, death, tears and sadness no longer exist. I have faith and hope in such an eschatological future. What I am arguing against is the ways in which such an eschatological vision is weaponized to minimize and belittle suffering and trauma in our present lives, as if our present lives are not important in God's 'grand scheme'.

Ultimately, this kind of toxic hope acts as a denial of real-life experience. It is not particularly interested in how you, the trauma survivor, feels. Rather it is focused on brushing aside your experience in favour of Scripture or lines from worship songs. It is not interested in listening to you but is more interested in hearing its own voice declare God's providential hand. Toxic hope is painful, dismissive, terrorizing and, worst of all, masked with faux kindness. Toxic hope wants to preserve its façade at the expense of your experience. Toxic hope kills.

Disruptions of hope

The experience of trauma is one that ruptures many of a person's strongly held beliefs and approaches to the world. Trauma disrupts doctrine and requires a different way of approaching theological categories such as hope.

Much of the traditional Christian discourse regarding hope rests on a linear understanding of both the life and death of Jesus and of the lives of people, in our case, trauma survivors. Jesus lives. Jesus suffers. Jesus dies. Jesus is resurrected victoriously. As we have already seen, this easy linear movement is dramatically disrupted by many theologians, both those interested in trauma and those who are not specifically.[13] Shelly Rambo disrupts this linear reading as she notes that in the experience of trauma, 'Death is not something concluded and life a fresh start and a new beginning.'[14] Life (or resurrection) is not always victorious, particularly in trauma experiences, and casting all our experiences in a resurrection light only serves to gloss over and do injustice to the realities of such experiences.

To return to the verse from Romans 5 that regards hope as a product of affliction, we find that trauma poses a serious challenge to this verse. While you may be able to argue (although I certainly would not) that some experiences of affliction do produce endurance, character, and ultimately hope, this is very difficult to argue in the experience of trauma. Trauma is not suffering, not run-of-the-mill affliction. It cannot be overcome by sheer bloody-mindedness. Flourishing in the aftermath of trauma requires, as we have been exploring already in this book, the beginning of an extended (possibly lifelong) process of self-remaking. Trauma cannot easily be substituted into this passage.

> The story doesn't necessarily alter the automatic physical and hormonal responses of bodies that remain hyper vigilant, prepared to be assaulted or violated at any time. For real change to take place, the body needs to learn that the danger has passed and live in the reality of the present.[15]

This perspective on trauma makes it clear that this is not something that can simply be 'overcome'. It is too simplistic a narrative to claim that such experiences necessarily (even in the case of suffering) produce perseverance, character, and ultimately hope. Our understanding of the psychology and physiology of trauma disrupts this scriptural perspective. While such progress is possible, it is rather an idealized perspective on what might be possible for those experiencing such 'afflictions'. If there is any boasting in such experiences, it is not of 'hope' but only of 'survival'.

This verse, among others, is a key example of the ways in which hope must be measured against real-life experience. We can be assured of our eschatological hope in Christ. We can be sure that, eschatologically, there is certainty of both salvation and eternal life in the kingdom of God. But if we are not to inflict further harm on those who have experienced trauma, it is essential that we take real life seriously. Real life disrupts hope. Denying real-life experience in favour of imagined hopeful future scenarios is dangerous. Thus, typical responses to the miscarrying person's experience, for example, 'You can always try again' or 'At least you know you can get pregnant', are some of the worst things to say in the aftermath of such experiences. Both statements are full of hope; the implication being that having become pregnant once you can (they hope) become pregnant again and next time (they hope) there would be a different outcome. Such hope is unfounded. It is unfounded in any kind of Christian understanding of what 'hope' might mean and what it is, particularly, that we have hope for and in. This kind of hope is not Godly, but simply optimism. Optimism is not hope. Moreover, such statements deny the real grief and distress at the current situation in the proposal of hope as a solution. Even if this turns out to be true and a second pregnancy is conceived and a child born, such statements minimize the real-life grief and distress that may come with the loss of a pregnancy. The conceiving of another baby does not cancel out the loss of the previous baby. As Miguel de la Torre notes in his critical reading of the story of Job:

> Job fathers seven new sons and two new daughters to replace those killed by Satan *on God's authority*. But children are not property where siring new ones can simply replace the old dead ones ... As any parent who has lost a child knows, no number of additional children can ever replace the loss of just one particular child.[16]

We might draw a parallel here with the narratives of crucifixion and resurrection in the Gospels. As we have already seen, the rush to the triumphal declarations of resurrection is emphatically rejected by many trauma theologians. Rambo, in particular, cautions against proclaiming resurrection and victory as a default position either in the pulpit or in the context of pastoral care. Of course, the resurrection does not occur until the horror, pain and absence of Good Friday and Holy Saturday have been endured. Rambo's challenge is to find ways in which we can slow or temper this journey to resurrection in order that these sites of pain, distress and disconnection might be given proper space within the Christian tradition. We might imagine the resurrection from the perspective of the disciples.[17] The small group of women and John who witnessed Jesus' crucifixion from the foot of the cross might very well be overjoyed at the resurrection of their dear friend and relative. But such joy does not cancel out the potentially traumatizing impact of witnessing such brutality and murder. It is easy to imagine that this group of people might continue to experience trauma symptoms – flashbacks, nightmares, hallucinations – long after the resurrection took place.

Rejecting triumphalist accounts of the cross is necessary if one is to do justice to the experience of trauma. Declaring Christ's victory over sin and death and hope in eternal life does not do justice to the real-life experience of the miscarrying person who experiences the miscarriage as trauma (or indeed, people who may have a multitude of other differing experiences of trauma).

Embracing hopelessness

In his work in *Embracing Hopelessness*, de la Torre unpicks the theological category of hope and disrupts it at a base level. He highlights the way in which this category of hope rests, theologically, on the concept of salvation history – a way of looking at the history of the world and seeing it as rooted in a divine purpose that is being outworked by God as the world moves towards a triumphal apocalyptic end of history. For de la Torre, such an understanding of the world is deeply rooted in the colonial quest and in 'a fundamentally European way of construing and relating to reality'.[18] Such Euro-centric history has been the prototype for salvation history – viewed as a movement towards utopia, ever-developing progress towards perfection. For the Christian, this is read as a sign of God's divine hand at work in the universe, but what if it 'is just a series of unrelated and unconnected events that occur in a nonlinear, disjointed, multidimensional passage of time? The disjointedness of history has led many of us to see patterns where none exists...'[19] Hope, in this context, is a denial of real-life experience. For anyone outside of the white North-Atlantic-centric theologians, embracing the traditional Christian narrative of hope requires a denial of 'their existential reality in exchange for the illusion of some dialectical movement toward a predominately white utopia that continues to exclude them in the here-and-now'.[20]

For de la Torre, drawing on both Foucault and Hegel, there is no grand narrative of salvation history. He concludes:

I find myself disagreeing with Martin Luther King Jr., who, quoting the nineteenth-century abolitionist, Rev. Theodore Parker, often said '[t]he arc of the moral universe is long, but it bends toward justice' (1986:52). The arc of the moral universe is *not* long, *nor does* it bend toward anything at all; because history lacks an arc, the universe is amoral, and an absence of salvation history means there is no bending toward justice. 'The cosmos,' according to Eagleton, 'is no more intent on improvement than it is hell-bent on self-destruction.' (2015: 97).[21]

While I have only engaged with his argument very briefly here, it is clear that applying a post-colonial methodology of deconstruction to articulations of salvation history reveals a very Euro-centric (and thus colonially implicated) approach to such history. De la Torre engages, in one of his chapters, with the Native American theologian Tink Tailor in order to see this 'history' from the perspective of Native Americans. The colonial influence on the way in which such history is read becomes immediately clear; this is no narrative of progress towards a utopia, but one of murder, genocide and oppression.

Once such an overriding concept of salvation history begins to be decolonized, it starts to beg the question of what, then, it might mean to hope. A destabilizing of the concept of salvation history does not eradicate the sense of eschatological hope that characterizes perspectives on eternal life. However, it does throw into question what hope there can be in this life. There is no bend toward justice built into the mechanism of the universe. What then does it mean to hope? Where does our hope lie? Perhaps we might have to now learn what it means to be hopeless.

There is, then, a possibility of hope. But this hope is not eschatologically focused but rather a kind of hope that is present-oriented and grounded in ethical action. Alongside this possibility of hope, we must hold, I argue, a sense of hopelessness. This sense of hopelessness rejects the triumphalism of the cross and rejects any easy assurances of the hope that may be found in Christ. While believing in an eschatological form of hope, this present hopelessness does not allow this future hope to overshadow the realities of the present lived experience of people.

This hopelessness is a praxis of resistance: 'Rather than accepting dominant narratives on the basis of fabled future utopias, praxis that is based on the lived experience and worldviews of the poor and dispossessed is a primary act of resistance.'[22] Rejecting easy turns to hope means that we approach God, as the sixth-century mystic Dionysius suggests, in a state of *unsaying*. Apophatic theology, of the sort Dionysius extols, traditionally understands this *unsaying* as that which is beyond words and thus often a silence. But here we might find other forms of unsaying that include cries that mirror that of Jesus on the cross where he cries out to God (Matt. 27.46 and Mark 15.34). There is paradoxical unsaying in this moment too, as Jesus perceives God as absent from him and yet cries out to God nonetheless (the speaking implying a presence in which God might hear this articulation). Hope and hopelessness overlap each other in this moment. Both are equally true and real, held in tension in an anguished cry of *unsaying*.

There is, I believe, a spiritual maturity on display in this cry out to God. Indeed, we see similar cries to God throughout the Scriptures. Consider Moses shaking his fist at God and asking God – accusing God – 'Why have you treated your servant so badly? Why have I not found favour in your sight?' (Num. 11.11). It is unhealthy to pretend all is well when we feel that God has broken God's promises to us, or that God has abandoned us at the time when we need God the most. It is unhealthy to pretend it is OK when we cry out to hear God's voice and yet God remains silent. There is a spiritual maturity in this open honesty and hopelessness that does not try to force itself into hope but rather holds its anger and forsakenness up for God to answer to.

If we accept the present reality and the lived experience of people who have been traumatized then we can become hopeless. This sounds negative but I do not mean it as such. In fact, in true apophatic style, I mean it, paradoxically, as an affirmation. We *can* become hopeless. For it is in hopelessness, in beginning from lived experience and not from a skewed sense of hope, that solidarity and action may be grounded. Rather than a Moltmannian sense of optimistic hope, grounded in an account of salvation history, we find an ethical hopelessness grounded in genuine solidarity. This kind of hopelessness rejects 'quick and easy fixes that temporarily soothe the conscience of the privileged'[23] in favour of solidarity and a praxis of liberation.

A spiritual practice of hopelessness: A praxis of resistance

What does a hopeless spiritual practice look like? I want to offer a suggestion, here, in two parts. First, if we take the theology of Miguel de la Torre seriously, then we must pray a prayer that goes something like, 'O God, this is hopeless. What, then, shall I do?' Like Moses, you may want to level some specific accusations at God. Do it. Say it out loud and let God hear it. Or maybe you want to use this prayer of hopelessness as a form of centring prayer in which the word 'hopeless' becomes the anchor word for a period of silent, centring and prayerful encounter with God.

I believe that the answer to this prayer will be different for each of us and possibly different for each of us at different times of our lives. But the specific forms of resistance that our hopelessness moves us into will be the second part of this practice of hopelessness. The revelation of what, therefore, we should do, that comes as a result of this prayer, is the embodied aspect of this practice – the hopelessness that moves us into action.

Beyond hopelessness?

Some kind of ethical hopelessness is, I think, a good thing to hold on to. It reminds us that while we do have an eschatological hope that is good and true, we also have an ethical imperative to take action to tackle the things that make us hopeless. So this might not be something you want or need to move on from.

But if you feel the need to balance this hopelessness out with something more hopeful, you might read the fortieth chapter of the book of Isaiah. The final verses read:

> Why do you say, O Jacob, and assert, O Israel,
> 'My way is hidden from God, and my right is disregarded by
>   my God'?
> Have you not known? Have you not heard?
> The Lord is the everlasting God, the Creator of the ends of
>   the earth.
> He does not faint or grow weary; his understanding is
>   unsearchable.
> He gives power to the faint, and strengthens the powerless.
> Even the youths will faint and be weary, and the young will
>   fall exhausted;
> but those who wait for the Lord shall renew their strength,
> they shall mount up with wings like eagles, they shall run
>   and not be weary,
> they shall walk and not faint.
> (Isa. 40.27–31)

God renews the strength of those who seek after Godself. Amen.

Notes

1 A version of this chapter was published in Karen O'Donnell, *The Dark Womb: Re-Conceiving Theology through Reproductive Loss* (London: SCM Press, 2022).
2 Rebecca Yarros, *Fourth Wing* (London: Piatkus, 2023), p. 130.
3 Margaret Adam, *Our Only Hope: More than We Can Ask or Imagine* (Eugene, OR: Pickwick Publications, 2013), p. 133.
4 Jürgen Moltmann, *The Experiment Hope*, trans. M. Douglas Meeks (London: SCM Press, 1975), pp. 57–8.
5 Adam, *Our Only Hope*, p. 75.
6 David Elliot, *Hope and Christian Ethics* (Cambridge: Cambridge University Press, 2017), p. 2.
7 Elliot, *Hope and Christian Ethics*, p. 61.
8 Karl Marx, *Introduction to A Contribution to the Critique of Hegel's Philosophy of Right*, 3 vols. (New York, 1976).
9 That is, Christians sometimes feel led to remind other Christians of these verses as an encouragement and sometimes as a reprimand.
10 Dholakia Uptal, 'What's the Difference Between Optimism and Hope? | Psychology Today United Kingdom', *Psychology Today* (blog), 26 February 2017, https://www.psychologytoday.com/gb/blog/the-science-behind-behavior/201702/whats-the-difference-between-optimism-and-hope, accessed 28.06.2024.
11 Terry Eagleton, *Hope Without Optimism* (New Haven, CT:Yale University Press, 2019), p. 114.
12 Eagleton, *Hope Without Optimism*, p. 4.
13 Walter Brueggemann, 'Reading from the Day "In Between"' in *The Shadow of Glory: Reading the New Testament after the Holocaust*, ed. Tod Linafelt (New York: Routledge, 2002), pp. 105–39; Alan Lewis, *Between Cross and Resurrection: A Theology of Holy Saturday* (Grand Rapids: Wm. B. Eerdmans Publishing, 2001).
14 Shelly Rambo, *Spirit and Trauma: A Theology of Remaining* (Louisville, KY: Westminster John Knox Press, 2010), p. 6.
15 Bessel van der Kolk, *The Body Keeps the Score: Mind, Brain and Body in the Transformation of Trauma* (St Ives: Penguin, 2015), p. 21.
16 Miguel A. De La Torre, *Embracing Hopelessness* (Minneapolis, MN: Fortress Press, 2017), p. 81. Italics in original.
17 Indeed, I have just done this in Karen O'Donnell, 'Surviving Trauma at the Foot of the Cross', in *When Did We See You Naked? Jesus as a Victim of Sexual Abuse*, ed. Jayme R. Reaves, David Tombs and Rocío Figueroa (London: SCM Press, 2021). pp. 260–77.
18 De La Torre, *Embracing Hopelessness*, p. 25.
19 De La Torre, *Embracing Hopelessness*, p. 58.
20 De La Torre, *Embracing Hopelessness*, p. 49.
21 De La Torre, *Embracing Hopelessness*, p. 59. Italics in original.
22 De La Torre, *Embracing Hopelessness*, p. 31.
23 De La Torre, *Embracing Hopelessness*, p. 139.

5

The Practice of Taking Action

> Every man of humane convictions must decide on the protest that best suits his convictions, but we must all protest.[1]

The last decade (2013–2023) has seen some of the largest and most consistent practices of protest across the world. From countless teenagers walking out of their schools in protest over climate change inaction, to massive Women's Marches complete with pussy hats, to Black Lives Matter protests, to an increase in strike action across multiple industries including teaching, commerce, hospitality, film-making and transport (to name just a few), the last few years have been an era of protest.

People are moved to take action when they feel their voices are not being heard, when their stories are not being believed, when their concerns go unacknowledged, and when those in power have no discernible interest in challenging the status quo. Forms of protest can differ dramatically. In my own profession of teaching, protests can range from standing on a picket line with a placard, or marching to places of governance to make dissatisfaction clear, to quieter forms of protest. This might be a marking and assessment boycott, where union members refuse to participate in grading student assignments, or 'action short of a strike'.

Action short of a strike is, weirdly, one of my favourite forms of protest. Not that I don't enjoy a good picket line or rally, but action short of a strike, such as 'work to rule', really hammers home the point. When teachers are called to 'work to rule' by their unions this means they only work their paid hours and only undertake responsibilities that are specifically in their job description. The reason I like it is that it makes clear, in teaching at least, how far above and beyond most teachers go in their everyday commitment to being a good teacher. It makes clear how much extra we were already doing. No lesson prepped for today? Well, I worked to rule and finished work when you stopped paying me so we're watching a video today. No marking done for this class? Sorry, senior leader, I worked to rule and so didn't spend three more hours of my own time marking students' work. I like it because it makes the point and it quickly becomes unsustainable. A strike day can come and go but a school or university (or any institution really!) cannot last long with staff working to rule.

I've been on strike a few times in my life as a working professional, and I have also taken part in political rallies both as a university student and more recently. This has been in protest against things like the invasion of Iraq, Brexit and the limitation of women's bodily autonomy. In each case, a feeling of hopelessness (see the preceding chapter) and of desperation has motivated me to action. I felt I had to do something – although, in doing something not much changed, politically at least. Teachers are still underpaid and overworked, Brexit still happened, the invasion of Iraq was only the tip of the iceberg, and don't get me started on women's bodily autonomy. But the protesting helped with my sense of hopelessness and desperation, with the sense that my voice was unheard.

In a different context, one of the contributing factors to my own post-traumatic remaking after my experiences of multiple pregnancy losses[2] was a sense of my academic writing in the area of reproductive loss and theology as a 'survivor's gift'. One of the ways in which I found my voice, took control of my narrative, shifted my self-perception and deepened my faith was by becoming very vocal about my experiences. I wrote about them extensively, I did lots of podcasts, I posted lots of links to charities, resources and agencies on my social media accounts. I have endometriosis and I make a point of talking regularly about my experiences of debilitating period pain, nausea, exhaustion and infertility. Why? Because it takes, on average, seven years for someone to get a diagnosis of endometriosis and they will regularly have to become their own fiercest advocate in order to get a diagnosis and any subsequent treatment. I talk about it all the time so people don't have to go through what I went through.

The benefits of engaging in protest and activism

It turns out I am not the only person who has found protest and activism to be significant in my own post-traumatic remaking. Research has clearly demonstrated that avoidance-based coping mechanisms (where people try to avoid any mention of their trauma) lead to higher psychological distress, PTSD symptoms, and a slower rate of trauma recovery. In comparison, approach-based strategies lead to faster recovery.[3] There is a well-established positive link between activist identity and psychological well-being.[4] Putting on a pussy hat with a million other women and fighting the patriarchy makes you feel better! Who knew?!

There are a number of reasons for this positive association. In their work with a range of survivors of sexual assault, Charlotte Strauss Swanson and Dawn M. Szymanski noted a series of positive benefits acknowledged by the survivors they worked with. This included the idea that involvement in activism (which took a diverse range of forms) had helped to facilitate a personal transformation: a liberated and renewed sense of self, a stronger sense of freedom and empowerment, a sense of control in their lives, the development of a stronger critical consciousness, an empowering shift in self-perception, interpersonal growth and healing, and the improvement of relationships.[5] They argue that research has shown 'that following a trauma, survivors often take part in behaviours such as volunteering and helping others, and that these behaviours encourage resiliency, well being, and in some cases, posttraumatic growth'.[6]

Of course, such a positive experience is not without risk. Some of Strauss Swanson and Syzmanski's participants indicated that engaging in this kind of protest and activism was, at times, triggering. They risked being overwhelmed and some felt burnt out by their involvement in these kinds of project.[7] Nonetheless, it is worth considering how collective action might contribute to a survivor's process of post-traumatic remaking, recognizing that activism can take a variety of forms and that there is great power in collective healing.

Biblical accounts of protest and action

Protest might not be the first thing that comes to mind when you think about the biblical text. However, once you start to look for it, elements of protest are relatively frequent. For example, a number of the psalms include elements that can be read as protest. We could consider Psalm 44. This begins with an account of the goodness of God towards the people. Verses 1–8 recount God's victory and steadfastness but in verse 9, the psalm takes a turn: 'Yet you [God] have rejected us and shamed us, and have not gone out with our armies.' The rest of the psalm is one of protest in which the psalmist lays out the multiple ways in which God has let the people down.

> You have made us like sheep for slaughter,
> and have scattered us among the nations.
> You have sold your people for a trifle,
> demanding no high price for them.
> You have made us the taunt of our neighbours,
> the derision and scorn of those around us.
> You have made us a byword among the nations,
> a laughing-stock among the peoples.
> All day long my disgrace is before me,
> and shame has covered my face
> at the words of the taunters and revilers,
> at the sight of the enemy and the avenger.
> All this has come upon us, yet we have not forgotten you,
> or been false to your covenant. (Ps. 44.11–17)

We find in this psalm direct accusations against God, the casting of God as the main foe of the people, an oppositional structure of the psalm in which the juxtaposition of praise and complaint emphasize the discord portrayed, and – through intertextual connections with Psalm 37 – a theme of divine neglect and injustice.[8] The psalm goes on to tell of the faithfulness of the people in the face of what they perceive as God's indifference or abandonment of them. Each verse could read like a protest placard, an explanation of why we are unhappy and what we expect to be done about it.

In the New Testament, we could consider the Magnificat as an example of protest. Recounted in Luke's Gospel and attributed to Mary as her song of praise, the Magnificat is a great example of a protest song. Mary sings:

> He [God] has shown strength with his arm;
> he has scattered the proud in the imagination of their hearts.
> He has brought down the powerful from their thrones,
> and lifted up the lowly:
> he has filled the hungry with good things,
> and sent the rich away empty.
> (Luke 1.51–53)

Benwildflower.com.
Used with permission from the artist.

None of these things has happened yet, but with the Incarnation of Christ, the kingdom of God is being ushered in. Mary sings these words as a prophetic protest in which she claims the future she believes she will see. I am always perplexed at the twee way in which the Magnificat is spoken or sung in Anglican evensong – soft and gentle, as if it is not a call for revolution and the overthrow of evil systems that exploit the poor and marginalized. Ben Wildflower's now famous screen print of the Magnificat helps us to remember the revolutionary tones of this protest song.

It is perhaps no surprise then that some of the readiest biblical forms of protest (the Psalms and the Magnificat) are also musical. Music has long been used to raise the profile of political issues or articulate a hopeful vision of the future. Music has played a rich part in the history of protest. This dates back centuries, but we can see it even in consideration of just the twentieth and twenty-first centuries. The spiritual songs of the African American community became songs of protest against slavery and were richly utilized during the campaign for civil rights in the United States. The Vietnam War era saw plenty of anti-war songs decrying the violence of war and hoping for peace, for example 'Peace Train' by Cat Stevens and 'Blowin' in the Wind' by Bob Dylan. More recently, one could point to the guerilla-style performances of the Russian feminist punk band Pussy Riot or even the chilling 'This is America' by Childish Gambino as forms of protest songs and performances, both of which are calling their respective countries to account for their failings.

Perhaps an unexpected biblical song to consider in this context is the Song of Songs. This biblical narrative is more often associated with love, romance and poetry than it is with songs of protest. However, a number of biblical scholars have explored the text in this way. Black and womanist scholars have read specific sections of the Song as a protest. For example, Robert Wabyanga has posited that Song of Songs 1.5–7 should be 'read creatively as an intellectual protest against racial injustices'.[9]

> I am black and beautiful, O daughters of Jerusalem,
> like the tents of Kedar; like the curtains of Solomon.
> Do not gaze at me because I am dark, because the sun has
>   gazed on me.
> My mother's sons were angry with me; they made me keeper
>   of the vineyards,
> but my own vineyard I have not kept!
> Tell me, you whom my soul loves, where you pasture
>   your flock,
> where you make it lie down at noon;
> for why should I be like one who is veiled beside the flocks
>   of your companions?

Wabyanga reads the unnamed female main character's declarations that she is 'black and beautiful' as a protest against dominant conceptions of beauty (which we must assume were that lighter skin was more beautiful). He draws this declaration into dialogue with similar statements by well-known Black civil rights leaders: 'Stephen Biko in his "Black is beautiful" campaign during the anti-apartheid protests of South Africa and Martin Luther King, Jr. who cried out, "Yes I am black and proud of it! I am Black and Beautiful!".'[10] These verses from the opening of the Song carry within them a protest around narratives that dominate beauty standards, racism and patriarchy.

But it is possible to read the Song as a whole as a form of protest. The biblical scholar Jimmy Loader notes the positioning of the Song of Songs in the genre of Wisdom literature alongside texts such as Ecclesiastes, Proverbs and Job. He argues that all Wisdom literature can be read as protest literature, to which we must assume the inclusion of the Song of Songs.[11] Michael Rea uses his own reading of Lamentations and Job to argue that:

> God not only tolerates pious lament and protest, but both authorizes and validates even some instances of *impious* protest – protest whose primary and most salient motivation is outright anger, despair, or similar affective states in response to the apparent injustice, wrongness or unlovingness of God's behaviour, and which is neither expressive of nor significantly motivated by faith or hope in God's love or goodness.[12]

Rea points to sections of the book of Job where Job angrily protests against God (Job 7.11–20) and outrightly accuses God (Job 30.16–23), which he highlights as impious protests. It is God's final word at the end of the book, indicating that Job alone has spoken rightly of God (Job 42.8), that is read as God's implicit validation of these impious protests.

This equation of Wisdom literature with narratives of protest might be easier to see in texts such as Job or Ecclesiastes – indeed Loader points to both of these texts as being pessimistic and having a critical spirit[13] – but what of the Song of Songs?

Jannie Hunter takes up this proposition and argues that the

Song represents the refutation of the normal in Israelite social consciousness and wisdom teaching. She positions the text of the Song in contrast to that of Proverbs which also deals with sexual intercourse. She writes: 'As it stands, the theme of the Song of Songs stands out distinctively in the canon and may well represent a protest against prevailing attitudes about love in the patriarchal society in which it was produced.'[14] She characterizes the Song as one that stands out for its 'positive stance on the woman's attitude to seeking, flirting with, longing for, and even having sex with the man'.[15]

In the 1990s, S. D. Goitein famously made the case that the Song of Songs was a text written by a woman.[16] There is certainly compelling, if not quite decisive, evidence that this might be so. In which case, considering the text as a protest becomes even more intriguing. It becomes, in a society in which women are not permitted to speak openly, a demonstration against prevailing social constructs.[17] In fact, the things that the Song celebrates are the very things that have been criticized by the prophets.[18]

The Song celebrates sexual attraction and arousal, so we can juxtapose Song 4.9ff. – 'You have ravished my heart, my sister, my bride, you have ravished my heart with a glance of your eyes, with one jewel of your necklace...' – with the command in Proverbs 6.25 – 'Do not desire her beauty in your heart and do not let her capture you with her eyelashes.' Similarly, the Song also revels in pleasure and indulgence. Song 1.2 reads, 'Let him kiss me with the kisses of his mouth! For your love is better than wine...' We can read this in direct contrast to Proverbs 21.17 'Whoever loves pleasure will suffer want; whoever loves wine and oil will not be rich.' Furthermore, the erotic language of the Song celebrates the pleasures of flirtation and sexual desire with no language around the honouring of virginity or purity as a metaphor for faith and adherence to the covenant.[19] Nakedness, in the Song, is not shameful but a celebration of the beauty of bodies, in direct contrast to the presentation of nakedness throughout the Hebrew Bible (e.g. the Genesis narrative, Leviticus 18, or Lamentations 1.8 in which nakedness is used as a direct metaphor for sinfulness).[20] What a contrast we find here! The Song is certainly doing something different. As well as the text itself forming a protest against prevailing standards of beauty, love and relationships (among lots of other things), we have to consider why it is included in the collection of texts that form the Bible in the first place. The Song contains no features that would usually be requisite for inclusion in the Bible. It contains no reference to God or description of any religious practices. Hunter concludes that maybe:

> The Song of Songs was included in the Canon for its stance on what was lacking in the religious corpus. It was included to fill a gap and to show that many of the other views in the Bible are not the complete truth about life. To protest positively against certain traditional views about women, love, relationships, physical beauty, and many other matters.[21]

So perhaps we can see both the text itself, and its inclusion in the canon, as forms of protest.

The Song of Songs as a spiritual (protest) text

Why is this significant? For centuries, the Song of Songs has been a text at the heart of the Christian spiritual tradition. Generations of spiritual seekers – including Origen, Bernard of Clairvaux and John of the Cross – have turned to the Song as a way of understanding what it means to seek after God and to encounter the divine. Bernard wrote 20 sermons just on the first verse of the Song – 'Let him kiss me with the kisses of his mouth'! The text has been, for a long time, a centrepiece of the Christian spiritual tradition although it has sadly fallen out of popularity in spirituality terms over recent years, perhaps due to a puritanical discomfort with the Song's erotic imagery, or because those who insist on literal readings of biblical narrative find themselves at a loss to know what to do with the text that includes erotic descriptions of intercourse between an unmarried couple, and a rape scene.

THE PRACTICE OF TAKING ACTION

What might it mean in terms of our spiritual lives, our seeking after God, to see the Song of Songs – this centrepiece of the Christian spiritual tradition – as a song of protest? If we read the text allegorically (which one has to do if one wants to see the text as being related to Christian spirituality at all) then it becomes possible to argue that a primary way in which we encounter the divine is through protest. Not the only way, but certainly an important way.

Engaging in protest and action requires a certain amount of faith. If you take to the streets to march for abortion rights, you must in some way believe that your action might make a difference. If you join a support group for a specific cause then, again, you must believe that what you're doing might matter and that things might change. The same is true of a spiritual practice of protest – to protest against God requires a belief in God, a belief that God might hear your protest, see your action, and be moved to act differently.

We see evidence of protest throughout the Scriptures. These can be small instances of implicit protest in the questions asked of God. Or they can be the more overt examples that we have encountered in this chapter. We see forms of protest that are not just questions but actions as well. The leaders of the first Christian community protested against forms of social inequality and injustice by ensuring that all members of the community were cared and provided for: 'All who believed were together and had all things in common; they would sell their possessions and goods and distribute the proceeds to all, as any had need' (Acts 2.44–45). In his discourse on the body in his letter to the Corinthians, Paul writes, in protest against the treatment of the vulnerable and marginalized, 'The members of the body that seem to be weaker are indispensable, and those members of the body that we think less honorable we clothe with greater honor, and our less respectable members are treated with greater respect' (1 Cor. 12.22–23).

Protest as a spiritual practice

As we turn towards considering what a spiritual practice of protest might look like, we can recognize that there is valuable benefit to the trauma survivor in taking part in forms of protest, whether that is a march or rally, or participating in social action. Both forms of protest can do us good and both forms of protest have strong grounding in the Christian tradition. Drawing on our engaging with the Song of Songs as a protest song, and given its centrality in the Christian spiritual tradition, I invite you to consider what it might mean to make protest – at least for a while – a central theme in your engagement with God.

This invitation leaves us with a few different options for thinking about a spiritual practice. Perhaps, most obviously, one could make one's spiritual practice a form of engagement in social action. Join a survivors' group. Join a campaign or pressure group. If you can't find one, then start one. Take your embodied experience of trauma and bring it into dialogue with others who have gone through similar things. Let your protest take the form of 'No one should have to go through what I went through' and make it happen! Let this be your protest to God at the same time. 'You who flung the stars into space and set the pattern of the tides and moon, you who know every hair on my head – I don't understand why what happened to me happened, but I'm not letting it happen to anyone else.'

You might like to make Sarah Corbett's 'Prayer of Lament' part of your practice of protest:

> Oh God, I get angry when I see people bullying others and abusing their power.
> I sink into sadness when I see people harming the world we are supposed to be stewards of.
> I'm disappointed in leaders for not being the best role models I want them to be.
> I'm even tempted to name, shame, blame, even throw something at them.

THE PRACTICE OF TAKING ACTION

Lord I want to be loving but I'm so quick to demonize power-holders and wish distress upon them.
And then ... I get angry with you God! You tell us to be gentle: how can I be watching people propping up suffering, inequality, environmental harm, the list goes on?!
Please help me.
Help my protests defuse conflict: when people raise their voice, help me lower mine. When others don't control their emotions help me stay calm.
Help my protests communicate love: help me avoid personal attacks. Instead of holding resentment let me offer forgiveness as fertile ground for progress.
Help my protests disarm critics: instead of being dismissive, help me be encouraging. Instead of being an aggressive enemy, help me be a critical friend.
Help my protests be persuasive: help me move from demanding to understanding. Instead of force, help me offer invitations to create the solutions together.
Help my activism be counter-cultural: when society wants a hero story rather than collective progress help me not succumb to ego-driven activism but act humble in service to the cause.
When people ridicule my gentle protests help me remember gentleness is a fruit of the Spirit and hold on to the effective gentle protesters before us: Abraham Lincoln's gentle voice, Dr King's tough mind and tender heart, Archbishop Tutu's forgiving and joyful soul...
Oh God help me be a gentle protester against injustice. I can't do this without you.
Amen.[22]

A different option in making protest your spiritual practice is to develop a protesting prayer. Formulating your own words of protest towards God might come naturally to you or might feel very foreign. You might feel this is not how you're 'supposed' to speak to God. But let us take our cue from Job's angry and impious protest prayers.

SURVIVAL

I cannot keep from speaking.
I must express my anguish.
My bitter soul must complain.
Am I a sea monster or a dragon that you must place me under guard?
I think, 'My bed will comfort me, and sleep will ease my misery.'
But then you shatter me with dreams and terrify me with visions.
I would rather be strangled – rather die than suffer like this.
I hate my life and don't want to go on living.
Oh, leave me alone for my few remaining days.
(Job 7.11–16, NLT)

And now my life seeps away.
Depression haunts my days.
At night my bones are filled with pain, which gnaws at me relentlessly.
With a strong hand, God grabs my shirt.
He grips me by the collar of my coat.
He has thrown me into the mud.
I'm nothing more than dust and ashes.
I cry to you, O God, but you don't answer.
I stand before you, but you don't even look.
You have become cruel toward me.
You use your power to persecute me.
You throw me into the whirlwind and destroy me in the storm.
And I know you are sending me to my death –
the destination of all who live.
(Job 30.16–23, NLT)

Words of Scripture. Validated by God as Job's right speaking. You can use these (and similar) words to bring your own protest to God for what has happened to you.

When is it time to move on?

If you start to feel burnt out and overwhelmed by engaging in this form of spiritual practice then it's time to move on, or at least time to press pause and take care of yourself. Protest and forms of action for social justice may continue to be important in your life at different times but if you're feeling burnt out then it's time for a different kind of practice. Perhaps moving away from direct, hands-on action to committed forms of intercession – either individually or corporately – might be a good move.

If you no longer feel as if you need to pray prayers of protest to God, perhaps it is time to move into something more peaceful, and still, and be able to dial down the trigger responses in your body. You might consider more contemplative forms of spiritual practice such as centring prayers or breath prayers (for which I definitely recommend Cole Arthur Riley's brilliant work *Black Liturgies*[23]). Both of these are practices that promote stillness and quiet alongside attention to one's body. Perhaps in this space you might know that God has heard your prayers of protest.

Notes

1 Martin Luther King, 'Beyond Vietnam: A Time To Break Silence' (Riverside Church, New York City, 4 April 1967), https://www.americanrhetoric.com/speeches/mlkatimetobreaksilence.htm, accessed 28.06.2024.

2 These experiences are more fully accounted in Karen O'Donnell, *The Dark Womb: Re-Conceiving Theology through Reproductive Loss* (London: SCM Press, 2022).

3 Rebecca Campbell, Emily Dworkin and Giannina Cabral, 'An Ecological Model of the Impact of Sexual Assault On Women's Mental Health', *Trauma, Violence & Abuse* 10, no. 3 (1 July 2009), pp. 225–46.

4 Charlotte Strauss Swanson and Dawn M. Szymanski, 'From Pain to Power: An Exploration of Activism, the #Metoo Movement, and Healing from Sexual Assault Trauma', *Journal of Counseling Psychology* 67, no. 6 (2020), p. 654.

5 Strauss Swanson and Szymanski, 'From Pain to Power', pp. 664–5.

6 Strauss Swanson and Szymanski, 'From Pain to Power', p. 655.

7 Strauss Swanson and Szymanski, 'From Pain to Power', p. 665.

8 Dalit Rom-Shiloni, 'Psalm 44: The Powers of Protest', *The Catholic Biblical Quarterly* 70, no. 4 (October 2008), p. 697.

9 Robert Kuloba Wabyanga, '"I Am Black and Beautiful": A Black African Reading of Song of Songs 1:5–7 as a Protest Song', *Old Testament Essays* 34, no. 2 (2021), p. 603.

10 Wabyanga, '"I Am Black and Beautiful"', p. 593.

11 J. A. Loader, 'Ecclesiastes' in *Dialogue with God: Preachers, Poets, and Philosophers*, ed. J. J. Burden and W. S. Prinsloo, The Literature of the Old Testament 3 (Cape Town: Tafelberg Publishers, 1987), pp. 50–1.

12 Michael C. Rea, 'Protest, Worship, and the Deformation of Prayer' in *Essays in Analytic Theology: Volume 2*, ed. Michael C. Rea (Oxford: Oxford University Press, 2020), p. 193.

13 Loader, 'Ecclesiastes', pp. 50–1.

14 Jannie Hunter, 'The Song of Protest: Reassessing the Song of Songs', *Journal for the Study of the Old Testament* 25, no. 90 (September 2000), p. 113.

15 Hunter, 'The Song of Protest', p. 114.

16 S. D. Goitein and Athalya Brenner, 'The Song of Songs: A Female Composition' in *The Song of Songs: A Feminist Companion to the Bible*, ed. Athalya Brenner and Carole Fontaine (Sheffield: Sheffield Academic Press, 1993), pp. 58–66.

17 Hunter, 'The Song of Protest', p. 115.

18 Othmar Keel, *The Song of Songs: A Continental Commentary*, trans. F. J. Graiser (Philadelphia, PA: Fortress Press, 1994), pp. 58–9.

19 Hunter, 'The Song of Protest', p. 120.

20 Hunter, 'The Song of Protest', pp. 121–2.

21 Hunter, 'The Song of Protest', p. 123.

22 Chine McDonald and Wendy Lloyd, *Rage and Hope: 75 Prayers for a Better World* (SPCK, 2021), pp. 68–70. Reproduced with permission of the Licensor through PLSclear.

23 Cole Arther Riley, *Black Liturgies: Prayers, Poems amd Meditations for Staying Human* (New York: Random House Publishing Group, 2024).

6

The Practice of Deconstruction

> True faith is a constant dialogue with doubt, for God is incomparably greater than all our preconceptions about Him; our mental concepts are idols that need to be shattered. So as to be fully alive, our faith needs continually to die.[1]

Deconstruction. It is a term that is having a bit of a moment in certain Christian circles. Depending on who you ask, it is either the epitome of evil or a necessary act of responsibility for those who profess to be Christian. You will find an abundance of podcasts that are exploring what it means to deconstruct your faith, which in turn have given rise to significant virtual communities of those who have deconstructed. Deconstruction can lead to the complete loss of faith or to the reconstruction of faith that has wrestled with the questions and doubts that have plagued the believer.

In this chapter, I am going to argue that the act of deconstructing one's faith can be a spiritual practice and one that is essential for the trauma survivor. Contrary to popular presentations of deconstruction as something that is evil, dangerous, anti-Scripture and anti-God,[2] I want to demonstrate that deconstruction is a work of the Holy Spirit and has a rich legacy in the Christian tradition. As the quote from the late Kallistos Ware that opens this chapter suggests, 'To be fully alive, our faith needs continually to die.'

What is deconstruction?

The word *deconstruction* is currently being used in two different ways. In an academic context, deconstruction is connected to the work of the philosopher Jacques Derrida; however, in popular Christian terms it is used to denote the critical examination of one's faith. The two concepts are connected and the contemporary work of deconstructing Christian faith has its roots in the ground work laid by Derrida in the mid-twentieth century.

Derridian deconstruction

Traditionally, and technically, deconstruction has been connected to the philosophy of Jacques Derrida developed in the late 1960s. For Derrida, deconstruction was 'a strategy for mindfully examining language, exposing (and subverting) the ways we discuss and practise truth and meaning – how we use binary language to smuggle in power dynamics that generate injustice'.[3] To deconstruct is to engage in critique and suspicion, initially of language but also of institutions.[4]

Such an approach to understanding the world around us has been criticized for being too negative and destructive.[5] However, Derrida himself acknowledges that negation on its own is inadequate. Deconstruction functions to remind us that every claim made is subject to revision and critique, but that does not mean that we should cease to make claims.[6] His critical deconstruction is 'implicitly affirmative'[7] as it opens up unexamined possibilities. It is not, as contemporary Christian critics of the deconstruction movement fear, simply destructive.

Popular Christian usage

The term *deconstruction* has, as I have already begun to indicate, taken on a popular life of its own and has become common parlance in the Christian context, especially with those who identify as ExVangelicals (people who have left evangelical churches and traditions). In her work with Christians who have deconstructed their faith, Olivia Jackson defines deconstruction as 'an intentional examination of one's core faith and beliefs, leading to a profound change in, or even loss of, that faith'.[8] Similarly, Aaron van Voorhis, an American pastor with a particular ministry to those who are deconstructing their faith, describes deconstruction as:

> A method of peeling back the layers of our religion in order to understand its ideological roots. Ultimately, it's about understanding that our theology, doctrine, beliefs, and practices are not some kind of black magic downloaded from God like software off the Internet, but a language of the soul that we came up with, a poetics that speaks of the ineffable and transcendent aspects of our experience.[9]

The goal of deconstruction is the process itself rather than any prescribed ending. For some who deconstruct, this might lead to a loss of their faith entirely and a complete move away from Christian institutions and structures. For others, deconstruction is often followed by periods of reconstruction and reconciliation. Van Voorhis again: 'It's important to understand that the goal of deconstruction is not destruction but a kind of reparation, a correction in the way we think about religion and participate in its structures.'[10]

The process of deconstruction is individual and will look different for everyone. But there is a general pattern that can be discerned. The process begins with the observation and recognition of the ways in which doctrines, creeds, traditions, beliefs and their effects are *constructed* and *interpreted* via communities rather than being the 'right' or 'only' way of thinking about things. This leads to critical analysis, engaging in educative activities, taking on varied interpretations and engagements, and attempts to seek out core nuggets of tradition and faith. The end result is, as already mentioned, rejection, reconstruction, and/or reconciliation.

Deconstruction and the Christian tradition

This work of deconstruction seems, in the analysis I have presented here, to be a distinctly modern thing, birthed in the mid-twentieth century and having a moment on social media, TikTok and podcasts. However, deconstruction is, I believe, deeply rooted in the Christian tradition. You do not have to look far to find historical examples of Christians engaging in critique of their faith and being transformed by the process. In this section, I offer three examples of the ways in which deconstruction can be understood as having form in the Christian tradition. First, I take two textual examples from the Christian mystic tradition – *The Cloud of Unknowing* and 'Dark Night of the Soul' – to examine the process and purpose of deconstruction within the Christian life. Finally, I briefly examine my own field of trauma theology as one in which the act of deconstruction is a necessity.

The Cloud of Unknowing

The Cloud of Unknowing is an anonymous fourteenth-century English text. Most likely written by a Carthusian priest living in the East Midlands to a lay believer, *The Cloud* is a guide to contemplative prayer written in the vernacular.[11] It is a pedagogical text, designed to initiate the reader into the spiritual practice of contemplative prayer, and is grounded in the tradition of the *via negativa*. The author writes that we can, through our senses, our imagination and our reason, know some things about God but that full knowledge of God is beyond human capacity; God is mystery. However, a bit like Derrida, the *Cloud* author does not want to leave us there in negation, but rather offers a pathway to full comprehension of God through the medium of love.

The *Cloud* author writes in chapter 3:

> For when you first begin ... all that you find is a darkness, a sort of cloud of unknowing: you cannot tell what it is, except that you experience in your will a simple reaching out to God.

THE PRACTICE OF DECONSTRUCTION

This darkness and cloud is always between you and your God, no matter what you do, and it prevents you from seeing him clearly by the light of understanding in your reason, and from experiencing him in sweetness of love in your affection. So set yourself to rest in this darkness as long as you can, always crying out after him who you love.[12]

This dark cloud stands between us and God, an impenetrable fog of 'unknowing'. It is here we find the hard limits of human understanding.[13] But this cloud can be pierced by 'a sharp dart of longing love'.

He [God] can be taken and held by love but not by thought. Therefore, though it is good at times to think of the kindness and worthiness of God in particular, and though this is a light and a part of contemplation, nevertheless, in this exercise it must be cast down and covered over with a cloud of forgetting. You are to step above it stalwartly but lovingly, and with a devout, pleasing, impulsive love strive to pierce that darkness above you. You are to smite upon that thick cloud of unknowing with a sharp dart of longing love. Do not leave that work for anything that may happen.[14]

This longing love, as I read it, is a stripping away of all the accoutrements of Christianity, all the baggage, all the preconceptions, all the painful nonsense that has been preached and professed. The one who seeks to find the truth beyond all this does so only by love. The only thing that is necessary is a love that longs to know the truth. I think the nature of this love is important too. It is a 'sharp dart', a small and spiky thing. It does not need to be big and bold. It does not need to pretend to be smooth and nice. It fits in the hand and is prickly. I feel this is a good description of what many of us are left with as we critically engage with our faith. Love. But small and spiky. Fortunately, this is, as the *Cloud* author tells us, all we need to encounter the Truth of God. There is also a persistence in here. The author tells us not to give up, not to leave this task for anything. Small, prickly, hard work. Sounds like deconstruction to me.

'Dark Night of the Soul'

Let us turn to another classic text in the Christian spiritual tradition, the sixteenth-century poem by John of the Cross – 'Dark Night of the Soul'. John was a Carmelite friar, mentored by Teresa of Avila. He was a reformer and a troublemaker! He was also, potentially at least, a trauma survivor. Those opposed to the reform movements Teresa and John were undertaking took John captive and imprisoned him. These captors were John's fellow Carmelite Brothers – not strangers, but those who had professed the same vows as John. His punishment included weekly (at least) public lashings and severe isolation in a tiny cell. This lasted for eight months. It was during this time that John wrote his most famous poem 'The Spiritual Canticle', as well as some other works. The 'Dark Night of the Soul' was written after his escape. A few years later, John wrote a commentary on the poem which was not completed before his death.

Like the term 'deconstruction', the phrase 'dark night (of the soul)' has found a different meaning from that originally intended by John. For John, the 'dark night' is 'a profound state of being-in-love: of being so intimately united with God – a God who can be neither understood nor fully known – that the individual is plunged into the darkness of this unknown'.[15] While, in modern parlance, we tend to use the phrase 'dark night (of the soul)' to indicate that someone is going through a particularly trying period that is, potentially, causing a crisis in faith, John uses the phrase quite differently.

John articulates three stages of a spiritual ascent – purgation, illumination, and union (these stages are common to many mystical writers). The dark nights occur in the transition from one stage to another (we will discuss stages of faith and transitions of crisis later on). In moving from purgation to illumination, the believer experiences a deep sense of dissatisfaction and affliction that may present itself as a crisis of faith.

This experience is the culmination of what may have been years of persistent commitment to growing in the ways of

God. What is happening here is a constitutive and fundamental reorientation of the personality structure. In the *dark night of the soul*, the individual can no longer sustain, in any way, comfortable illusions about who he or she is before others and before God: one stands naked before God and before oneself in this phase of the journey. John calls this a dark night since the natural light of one's own capacity to know and make sense of things no longer functions in any familiar way, and the light of God has not yet been revealed in its fullness.[16]

How do we move from one stage in our faith to another? Through the dark nights which are not crises of faith *necessarily*, but rather places of purging, dissatisfaction with the way things are, and a recognition of the emptiness within us. The spiritual director and psychotherapist Ellen Haroutunian suggests:

> What if we treated deconstruction as a type of 'dark night of the soul' à la John of the Cross? 'Dark night' implies nothing bad. Rather, it's a movement from what was once certain to a deeper knowing and deeper union with God. It does require letting go of much of what is old, and of attachments that hold us back and keep false personas in place.[17]

Deconstruction, in this perspective, is a necessary and vital part of our spiritual lives. It is part of how we move towards deeper connection and deeper union with God.

Trauma theology as deconstructive work

I believe that deconstruction is an essential part of post-traumatic remaking of the self for the trauma survivor. I have previously described trauma as something that rolls through our theological landscapes like an earthquake, uprooting our familiar landmarks and byways.[18] If one is to engage with the process of post-traumatic remaking then one will have to address why these landmarks of doctrine, creed, theology, belief and practice have fallen. Why did they not stand in the face of the experience of trauma? What is it that now needs to be revisited (or perhaps even attended to for the first time) in the aftermath of trauma? Similarly, Terri Daniel writes, specifically in the case of trauma that causes grief, that 'Trauma can shake the foundations of our cognitive, cultural, spiritual, and religious assumptions, successful coping of grief often requires a radical overhaul of these ideas.'[19]

Trauma theology is, I argue, a theology of deconstruction. This is why I usually situate my own work in the field of Constructive Theology. This methodological approach to the *doing* of theology necessarily requires an act of deconstruction – or an *undoing* – as it takes time to unpick the ways in which previous theologies have been constructed and to examine the ways in which such theologies have traditionally failed (usually) to do justice to the experiences of trauma and what is required of the trauma survivor in trauma's aftermath. Serene Jones and Paul Lakeland describe the work of constructive forms of theology like this:

> We are not interested in merely describing what theology has been; we are trying to understand and construct it in the present, to imagine what life-giving faith can be in today's world. In doing so, as with any construction job, we are attempting to build a viable structure. In our case, that structure is an inhabitable, beautiful, fruitful theology.[20]

This statement has been key for me in thinking about the kind of work I am doing. I see my work in trauma theology as an attempt to build theologies that we can live in and that bring us life. It is my contention that, after the experience of trauma, deconstruction of theology is often essential.

There are plenty of examples of this kind of deconstructive work in the field of trauma theology. In my own work reflecting on my experience of reproductive loss, I had to *undo* theologies of prayer, of hope, of providence, and of the body in order to make space for the constructive work that was necessary within my theology. How, I wondered, could I hold on to my faith in the aftermath of my trauma? Similarly, in her work with survivors of sexual abuse, Jennifer Beste deconstructs theologies of grace in order to make sense of concepts of free will and autonomy for trauma survivors.[21] Again, various scholars have deconstructed the theology and practice of the Eucharist as a site in which trauma is particularly entangled.[22]

Suffice to say, deconstruction has a long legacy within the Christian tradition. It is not antithetical to the Christian faith. It is not something to fear but rather an essential part of the Christian life.

Deconstruction and spiritual growth

As an essential part of the Christian life, and particularly of spiritual development, we find these experiences of deconstruction articulated in the literature on faith development and spiritual growth. In Evelyn Underhill's work on mysticism, she synthesizes stages of mystical development that she finds in her analysis of a wide range of mystical texts. She names these as:

- Awakening of Self.
- Purgation of Self.
- Illumination.
- Dark Night of the Soul.
- The Unitive Life.[23]

We see here the familiar three stages so common throughout the literature in Christian spirituality, those of purgation, illumination, and union. But these are rearranged to indicate that between each distinctly positive stage (now awakening, illumination, and union), there is a challenge – in the first case that of purgation of the self, and in the second, that of a dark night. Underhill writes that when one's sense of equilibrium is disturbed (perhaps through a trauma experience, we might suggest), it can result in a 'shifting of the field of consciousness from lower to higher levels ... the necessary beginning of any process of transcendence'.[24] These periods of deconstruction (to use a term unfamiliar to Underhill) are essential parts of our spiritual lives.

Perhaps the most famous contemporary work on faith development was undertaken by James Fowler in his large-scale survey of stages of faith. Fowler posits seven stages of faith development. Drawing on cognitive development theories, the first four stages are age related:

0 – Undifferentiated Faith (0–2 years).
1 – Intuitive-Projective Faith (2–7 years).
2 – Mythic-Literal Faith (7–12 years).
3 – Synthetic-Conventional Faith (12+ years).

The remaining levels have been articulated with age ranges attached to them but these are largely unhelpful and so I have not included them here.

4 – Individual-Reflective Faith.
5 – Conjunctive Faith.
6 – Universalizing Faith.

While this research is not without its problems (not least the lack of diversity within the sample group), Fowler has indicated the challenge of transition that Underhill noted 80 or so years before him:

> Many people hover indefinitely between stages 3 and 4 because it is more difficult to make changes when relationships, habits, patterns, and lifestyles have been firmly established. For many people, the transition from Stage 3 to Stage 4 never happens.[25]

Stage 3 is characterized by conformity to authority. Fear plays a significant part in this stage: fear of the unknown and fear of any conflicts with one's beliefs. Such conflicts are suppressed in preference for maintaining the status quo. Stage 4 is the stage in which the individual takes personal responsibility for their faith and beliefs. Here there is an openness to the complexity of faith. Subsequent stages require comfortableness with mystery, paradox and transcendence. In this reading of the stages of faith development, we can posit that deconstruction is necessary for any progress beyond stage 3 in Fowler's terms.

A work of the Holy Spirit

Might, then, we see deconstruction as a work of the Holy Spirit? The Spirit who is akin to Lady Wisdom in the Wisdom tradition, she who brings us into unity with Divine, she through whom we are born again? Through the Holy Spirit we die and are born again – a purgation of who we once were and a bringing into new life. As Lady Wisdom we encounter one who brings us to an awakening of the self, an illumination of truth, beauty, and goodness, along with godly living. And it is the Holy Spirit that brings Christians into unity. Paul exhorts the Ephesians, 'Make every effort to keep yourselves united in the Spirit' (Eph. 4.3), and to the Corinthians he writes 'we have all been baptized into one body by one Spirit' (1 Cor. 12.13).

A spiritual practice of deconstruction

What then is our spiritual practice in terms of deconstruction? You are probably doing some of this deconstructive work already, either consciously or not. You may have already found communities of deconstructing people in digital spaces like Nomad, or at festivals like Greenbelt and Wild Goose. It is important to remember that while this might feel like a very cerebral activity, it is an activity that we undertake in our body. The process of deconstruction might also require learning to trust our gut when we encounter the theologies, narratives and interpretations that are life-giving and inhabitable for us. This can be challenging when we have been taught that our bodies are things to be subdued and dominated, and that are ultimately not trustworthy. Richard Rohr tells us that we do not think ourselves into new ways of living; we have to live ourselves into new ways of thinking.²⁶ My hope is that this spiritual practice of deconstruction might be an embodied way that allows us to live ourselves into new, fruitful, life-giving and inhabitable theologies.

Movement makes meaning

When I studied for my Master's degree, I used to swim regularly, enjoying the physical movement of my body in contrast to the hours of studying at my desk and attending lectures and seminars. While swimming, my brain had space to run free and I would often find the answers that I had been seeking in my research – answers and intuitions and ideas that had eluded me in the library or at my desk – bubbling up within my body as I swam. I used to keep a notebook in my swimming bag so I could quickly write these down before they drifted away. The movement of my body created space for meaning.

Think about how you like to move your body. Think without judgement, without concern for 'proper' ways or 'proper' equipment. How do you like to move your body? Is it dance? Is it a walk to a coffee shop for a cappuccino? Is it yoga? Is it running? I'm immediately reminded here of the *Friends* episode where Rachel is embarrassed by Phoebe's wild and joyful style of running. That is, until she has a go at it herself and revels in the way her body moves. Is it swimming? Is it hiking? Is it gardening? How does your body like to move?

Whatever way your body likes to move, let it. And as you do, allow yourself to enjoy it. Let it bring you alive.

Let this joyful movement be a space in which you can create and encounter meaning. Bring your questions, your confusion, the layers of your faith that you are peeling away. Let them flit through your mind as you move and let the physical movement of your body create a space in which theologies grow and come to life. Let the Holy Spirit move in you. She is busy. Let Lady Wisdom join you in your movement, making space for wisdom to bubble up inside your body.

I think this is a practice that we would all benefit from

throughout our lives. Making a regular space for joyful movement of our bodies that creates space for meaning-making is a lifelong practice that not only aids in the kind of deconstructive work we have been exploring here, but also enables us to encounter our bodies with joy and freedom, to learn to trust our guts, and to move with the Holy Spirit.

Notes

1 Kallistos Ware, *The Inner Kingdom: Volume 1 of the Collected Works* (Crestwood, NY: St. Vladimir's Seminary Press, 2001), p. 29.

2 Alisa Childers, 'Why We Should Not Redeem "Deconstruction"', *The Gospel Coalition* (blog), 18 February 2022, https://www.thegospelcoalition.org/article/redeem-reconstruction/, accessed 28.06.2024.

3 Bradley Jersak, *Out of the Embers: Faith After the Great Deconstruction* (New Kensington, PA: Whitaker House, 2022), p. 19.

4 Steven Fekete and Jessica Knippel, 'The Devil You Know: An Exploration of Virtual Religious Deconstruction Communities', *Journal of Religion, Media and Digital Culture* 9, no. 2 (23 October 2020), p. 169.

5 See, for example, Rita Felski, *The Limits of Critique* (Chicago, IL: University of Chicago Press, 2015).

6 David Newheiser, *Hope in a Secular Age: Deconstruction, Negative Theology and the Future of Faith* (Cambridge: Cambridge University Press, 2019), p. 18.

7 Newheiser, *Hope in a Secular Age*, p. 22.

8 Olivia Jackson, *(Un)Certain: A Collective Memoir of Deconstructing Faith* (London: SCM Press, 2023), p. xvi.

9 Aaron Van Voorhis, *A Survival Guide for Heretics* (Wipf and Stock Publishers, 2016), p. xii.

10 Voorhis, *A Survival Guide for Heretics*, p. xiii.

11 Stephen Chase, 'Anonymous (Fourteenth Century): The Cloud of Unknowing' in *Christian Spirituality: The Classics*, ed. Arthur Holder (London: Routledge, 2010), p. 161.

12 Anonymous, *The Cloud of Unknowing*, ed. James Walsh, Classics of Western Spirituality (New York: Paulist Press, 1981), pp. 120–1.

13 Jersak, *Out of the Embers*, p. 99.

14 Anonymous, *The Cloud of Unknowing*, pp. 130–1.

15 David B. Perrin, 'John of the Cross (1542–91) The Dark Night' in *Christian Spirituality: The Classics*, ed. Arthur Holder (Routledge, 2010), pp. 221–2.

16 Perrin, 'John of the Cross', p. 226.

17 Personal Correspondence cited in Jersak, *Out of the Embers*, p. 98.

18 Karen O'Donnell, *Broken Bodies: The Eucharist, Mary and the Body in Trauma Theology* (London: SCM Press, 2018).

19 Terri Daniel, 'Grief as a Mystical Journey: Fowler's Stages of Faith Development and Their Relation to Post-Traumatic Growth', *The Journal of Pastoral Care & Counseling* 71, no. 4 (2017), p. 220.

20 Paul Lakefield and Serene Jones, eds, *Constructive Theology: A Contemporary Approach to Classical Themes* (Minneapolis, MN: Fortress Press, 2005).

21 Jennifer Erin Beste, *God and the Victim: Traumatic Intrusions on Grace and Freedom* (Oxford: Oxford University Press, 2008).

22 See, for example, O'Donnell, *Broken Bodies*; Marcus Pound, 'Eucharist and Trauma', *New Blackfriars* 88, no. 1014 (2007), pp. 187–94; Dirk G. Lange, *Trauma Recalled: Liturgy, Disruption, and Theology* (Minneapolis, MN: Fortress Press, 2010).

23 Evelyn Underhill, *Mysticism* (New York: Doubleday, 1990).

24 Underhill, *Mysticism*, p. 176.

25 Daniel, 'Grief as a Mystical Journey', p. 226.

26 Richard Rohr, 'Journey to the Center', *Center for Action and Contemplation* (blog), 28 December 2015, https://cac.org/daily-meditations/journey-to-the-center-2015-12-28/, accessed 28.06.2024.

7

The Practice of Pleasure (yes, that kind of pleasure)

'Let him kiss me with the kisses of his mouth.' (Song of Songs 1.1)

Masturbation is a sin. It is unhealthy. It is selfish. It will make you go blind! It is probably quite easy to dismiss that last claim (although it was certainly a prevalent anxiety up until the mid-twentieth century), but for anyone raised in the Christian faith, you will have most likely encountered the former claims. Purity culture – rife in the latter part of the twentieth century and up into the present day – made it clear that all sexual things (impulses, urges and experiences) were to be kept only for heterosexual marriage. Masturbating before marriage (and even on one's own in marriage) was something sinful that needed to be repented.

Why?

Scripture has remarkably little specific to say about masturbation, in comparison with the big deal that is often made about it in Christian communities. The opening sentence in an online article about what the Bible says about masturbation reads, 'Let's be clear, masturbation is an act of instant, self-gratification. It is quite the opposite of the self-control that is taught in the Bible. Self-control is freedom from our passions, a gift from God, and a fruit of the Spirit (Gal. 5:22–23).'[1]

There is nothing directly about 'masturbation' in the Bible. If one wants to read prohibition against masturbation into the Bible text one has to do so through vague-ish verses about cleanliness, sexual immorality, lust, sexual impropriety and – as we see in the quotation above – self-control. A classic text that

Christian teaching often draws on in relation to masturbation is the Hebrew Bible narrative of Onan. In the text of Genesis 38, Onan is tasked by his father with impregnating his sister-in-law Tamar after the death of her husband (his brother Er). It would seem that Onan pulled out whenever he had sex with Tamar in order to avoid impregnating her, and 'spilled the semen on the ground'. This 'the Lord considered evil' (Gen. 38.9–10) and so God put him to death. Arguably, the reason God kills Onan is not because of some kind of connection with masturbation but rather to do with Onan's refusal to fulfil his socio-ethical and religious duty in impregnating his widowed sister-in-law. Nonetheless, masturbation is the lens through which this text has been read in the Christian tradition.

Similarly, the Hebrews referred to the text of Leviticus 15.16–17 in connection with masturbation: 'Whenever a man has an emission of semen, he must bathe his entire body in water, and he will be ceremonially unclean until the next evening. Any clothing or leather with semen on it must be washed with water, and be unclean until the evening.' The concept of uncleanness became associated with masturbation but no more so than with sexual intercourse. It was considered a minor ceremonial violation rather than a major sin.[2]

Nothing in the New Testament specifically discusses or prohibits masturbation. As I mentioned above, there are general prohibitions about sexual immorality and lust which have, in some types of Christianity at least, been read as prohibiting masturbation. But it is not that simple! And at least some of this Christian thinking is problematically grounded in Neoplatonic dualism. In this case, the body and the spirit are set in opposition to one another and so the body becomes something that must be conquered, controlled and subdued in order for more spiritual and holy things to come to the fore. The passions one feels are not to be trusted but rather subdued and killed in order for one's relationship with God (and with fellow Christians?) to flourish.

These texts from the Hebrew tradition were distorted by Christians so that the minor ceremonial violation of the emission of semen has become a major sin, and the death God inflicted on Onan has become conflated with the punishment for masturbation. This text was used by the early Church Fathers to prohibit and cast as sinful any sexual activity that was not for the purpose of procreation. Jerome writes, after citing the story of Onan: 'Does he [the heretic Jovinianus against whom Jerome is writing] imagine that we approve of any sexual intercourse except for the procreation of children?'[3] Similarly, John Calvin writes, 'It is a horrible thing to pour out seed besides the intercourse of man and woman.'[4]

A significant influence on the tradition of Christian thinking (and teaching) connected to masturbation stems from the work of Augustine. Prior to his conversion to Christianity, Augustine had been a Manichaean, a cult in which sex was associated with weakness of the body. The Manichaean command for celibacy was a profound and distressing challenge to Augustine, resulting in the crisis that ultimately prompted his conversion to Christianity, at which point he was able, finally, to live a chaste and celibate life.

Needless to say, this experience of sex, sexual desire, and the inability to conform to a celibate life profoundly coloured Augustine's thinking and teaching on sex. Sex, Augustine argued, was only permissible for procreation and, even then, only in the missionary position with the penis in the vagina. Both masturbation and any form of contraception were forbidden as contra to the *telos* of sex for procreation. Ironically, Augustine had more tolerance for prostitution than for masturbation for the unmarried man (obviously not for women!)! James A. Brundage, in his history of masturbation, notes that one ancient authority

> advised a person not engaged in marital sexual intercourse who felt a sexual climax coming on, to lie still, taking care to avoid touching the genitals, make the sign of the cross, and fervently pray beseeching God not to allow him or her to slip into orgasmic pleasure.[5]

The Hebrew tradition of classifying semen emission as unclean, alongside the killing of Onan by God for what was read (by

Christians) as a sin connected to semen emission, combined in early Christian teaching to produce a position in which anything sexual that did not take place between a heterosexual married couple for the purpose of procreation was sinful. The focus was primarily on the man – masturbation was sinful because it led to the emission of semen that was not for procreation. What a waste! Of course, this focus on masturbation is very one-sided. After all, for women, masturbation and orgasm have nothing to do with procreation.

Women's pleasure

There is a significant gender difference when it comes to orgasms, masturbation, and sexual pleasure, not least in terms of what is produced and released during an orgasm. For women, masturbation and orgasm are not connected to procreation. A woman can, of course, become pregnant without experiencing any sexual pleasure in the procreative act. And experiencing an orgasm is not, necessarily, synonymous with sexual satisfaction.[6]

Women's sexual satisfaction has been long hindered by the phallocentric approach to (hetero)sexuality that prioritizes the coital imperative (penis-in-vagina sexual intercourse) and the male orgasm. Vaginal-penile intercourse has long been considered the most natural, most quintessential, form of sex, sitting at the top of the hierarchy of sexual behaviours.[7] Similarly, the male orgasm has been understood as the pinnacle of sex. It signals the end of sex and has been perceived as more legitimate than women's orgasms perhaps because of its obviousness and visibility.[8] Sadly, the prioritizing of the coital imperative and the male orgasm has hindered, and continues to hinder, the experience of sexual pleasure and orgasm for women.

Research from 2014 asked women who have sex with men to talk about their perspective on and thoughts about masturbation. This research revealed the extent to which phallocentric sexual scripts had conditioned the ways in which women think about masturbation. These women described masturbation as an activity that threatens their partner's masculinity, or is something that is done for their partner's viewing pleasure, or is something that should only be done by men. In each of these responses we can see the ways in which women's pleasure (or lack thereof) is tied to men's sexual activity. Women sacrifice – consciously or unconsciously – their sexual satisfaction for men.

Recent research into women's sexual satisfaction and pleasure indicates that a more diverse repertoire of sexual behaviours (not just penis-in-vagina intercourse) and a focus on prioritizing one's own orgasms (for women) both lead to more frequent orgasms for women and greater sexual satisfaction. Both of these shifts in priority during sexual intercourse represent the challenging of male-oriented, phallocentric sexual scripts.

Trauma and sexual pleasure

For many traumatized people, including but not limited to those who have experienced trauma as a result of sexual assault, sexual violence, gender-based violence or purity culture, experiencing sexual pleasure may be very difficult. This can be a result of the disconnect with one's body that is often experienced by trauma survivors. This shut down, disconnect response to trauma is an automatic response in the face of a traumatic experience which 'our body has determined is our best chance to get through this [experience].'[9] Arguably, a society that 'celebrates bodily dissociation and mastery of physicality as a sign of maturity or status'[10] sets up the foundations for this kind of response to trauma. But when one is disassociated from one's body, sexual pleasure becomes a tricky thing. In some cases, the disconnection leads to a complete lack of interest in sex, an inability to connect with the body as a site of pleasure, and an inability to experience any kind of sexual pleasure through masturbation or partnered sexual activity. Alternatively, those who have experienced sexual assault as young people might find that 'they are more prone to automatic functioning (i.e. undertaking actions with little awareness) on a daily basis. This may hinder their ability to connect with their sexual self and, ultimately, to positively evaluate their sexuality (i.e., sexual satisfaction).'[11] Furthermore, some research with trauma survivors has indicated that post-traumatic stress symptoms are a predication of poor behaviour regulation which is, in turn, a predication of sexual risk-taking.[12] This means that the disconnect from the body often experienced by trauma survivors can mean that survivors disregard their own bodily safety and engage in risky sexual behaviours.

Masturbation and orgasms are good for your health

The third-century physician Galen prescribed masturbation for women in order to release the secretions he believed built up in women's bodies. Fifteen hundred years later, Victorian physicians provided both manual clitoral stimulation (until their arms ached!) and eventually built sex machines to bring women to orgasm. This was for the good of their health! Physicians prescribed 'hysterical paroxysm' (that is, orgasm) as a treatment for female hysteria. While this seems weird to our modern minds, I also want to argue that masturbation and orgasm is good for our spiritual health!

The benefits of masturbation and orgasm are widely documented. For everyone, masturbation should be considered medically healthy and psychologically normal. Despite what many Christians involved in purity culture might tell you, the existence of masturbation addiction has never been proven. Research has clearly demonstrated that masturbation improves sexual health and relationships, increases intimacy with partners, relieves depression, leads to a higher sense of self-esteem, lowers the probability of prostate cancer, reduces the chance of death from coronary heart disease, and, weirdly, helps you breathe better by reducing swollen nasal blood vessels. Orgasms release the hormones oxytocin, prolactin and endorphins which promote happiness and pleasure while reducing depression and anxiety. Specifically, women who masturbate have more frequent gynaecological examinations (reducing risks of cancer and other health issues), higher self-esteem, better sexual function with partners and better body image.

Sexuality and spirituality

Why am I talking about masturbation and orgasms in a book on spiritual practices for trauma survivors? First, as I mentioned earlier, the loss of sexual pleasure and dysregulation in sexual behaviours are common features of post-traumatic stress. I want to talk about masturbation as a practice that might enable trauma survivors to encounter their bodies in positive and healthy ways and to develop positive sexual self-image. As I have demonstrated already, masturbation can bring with it a multitude of health benefits both physical and psychological. Second, I argue that there is the potential for a spiritual health benefit in this practice too. Our spiritual lives should not be cut off from our sexual lives. Holistic approaches to spirituality are ones that take our embodied nature – replete with passions, emotions and orgasms – seriously. When we believe that sexual things are outside the realm of spirituality and our encounters with the divine, we create a framework in which sexuality becomes antithetical to spirituality and thus something to be ashamed of and for which we should feel guilty. Joy Bostic, in her work on spirituality and sexuality in Toni Morrison's *Beloved*, notes that:

> In contemporary culture, many Christians continue to believe that bodies and human sexuality are at war with who Christians aspire to be spiritually. There is fear and suspicion of the erotic, because in the history of the dominant Western culture, sex and the erotic are often depicted in violent and objectifying ways. This exploitation of sexuality causes many women, particularly women within marginalized cultures, to be protective of their sexuality. The problem is not sexuality and the erotic, in and of themselves, rather, sexuality and the erotic are often presented as disconnected from sacred spirit. Many Christian churches contribute to the problem by primarily addressing sexuality in prohibitive and shaming ways, leaving a void regarding how people can live out their sexualities in concert with their religious convictions. This separation of sexuality from spirituality results in alienation and hinders people from viewing sexuality positively.[13]

I want to give us opportunity to connect – or rather 'reconnect' – sexuality and the erotic to sacred spirit, as Bostic puts it. I use the term 'reconnect' here because, as any perfunctory survey of the Christian spiritual tradition will reveal, eroticism, sensuality and quasi-orgasmic experience has a rich history among the mystics.

Christian mysticism: erotic desire

Christian mysticism is rife with erotic discourse, imagery and experience. Indeed, the language of Christian mysticism is rooted in the sexy poem of the Song of Songs in the Hebrew Bible, as we encountered earlier in our chapter on protest. Space here does not permit a detailed analysis of the place of this erotic poem in Christian spirituality, but suffice to say the two are intimately connected.[14] The Song of Songs is a weird text to find in the Scriptures. It makes no mention of God or religious practice. It is a text that is dominated by the female voice in which the unmarried woman talks about how much she fancies her suitor and how much he turns her on. He, in turn, praises her beauty and tells her how much he wants to make love to her. There is, of course, a strong tradition of reading the text allegorically and seeing it as a discourse between the soul (the woman) and God (the bridegroom). The Song of Songs gives us pangs of compunction, sweet sensations of God's palpable presence, fleeting moments of ecstatic union with Christ as his bride, searing desire for God, and the soul's awareness of transformation through Christ's love, all of which are essential to the tradition of Christian spirituality. Jeanrond notes, 'The mystical discourse of love thus shows that the erotic and the sacred need not be understood in terms of radical opposition. Rather they have been experienced to be closely connected.'[15]

There are many examples throughout the Christian mystical tradition of mystics whose experience of the divine has a distinctly sexy mode. One such example is that of Rupert of Deutz (d. 1129) who was a Benedictine abbot. In a dream, Christ called him into a mutual kiss. Rupert kissed Christ on the mouth and Christ opened his mouth to allow Rupert to kiss him more deeply. Thirty days later, Rupert was in bed and felt the presence of a man above him. This man entered him and penetrated him to the core. Rupert felt a substance moving in his spiritual womb which he understood as the Holy Spirit. Not only are the sexual experiences in this mystical encounter clearly obvious, they are also gender fluid and homo-erotic. Rupert is penetrated by the male Divine (who Rupert understands as a 'man'). Rupert understands himself to become 'pregnant', indicating a gender fluidity at play in this experience. Sexuality and spirituality are not at odds but rather in symbiotic relationship, even partnership.[16]

Even in these brief examples we can see that spirituality and sexuality – sexual passions, sexual experiences – are intimately entwined and not antithetical to each other. Eros-infused spirituality seems to have taken a back seat after the Reformation but it is still there, in our Christian tradition, waiting to be rediscovered once again.

Sexual pleasure as a spiritual practice

The relationship between sexuality and spirituality is not exclusive to Christianity. Indeed, Hugh Urban notes that, 'Male–Female sexual differentiation and the act of sexual union are among the most pervasive, recurring and multivalent themes running through esoteric traditions…'[17] The union of male and female bodies in sex is a common metaphor for the ideal of divine union. Urban goes on to argue that:

> The symbolism of sexual union is one of the oldest tropes in Western esoteric literature, appearing throughout early Hermetic, Christian, and Jewish traditions alike to express the ineffable nature of the divine, the transmission of secret knowledge, and the experience of mystical union.[18]

Urban is particularly focused on heterosexual activity in religious traditions, although this is not exclusive and homosexual union also has the capacity to symbolize spiritual things in some traditions.

The African American thinker and writer Audre Lorde explores the place of the 'erotic' in her life and the ways in which it might be utilized in our lives. She positions the erotic as the intense kernel of our being that when released 'flows through and colours my life with the kind of energy that heightens and sensitizes and strengthens all my experience'.[19] The erotic is at the heart of who we are, it is at the foundation of our embodied experiences and encounters with the other and with the divine. As well as a strengthening and sensitizing energy, the erotic is also a powerful motivator. Lorde writes: 'Recognising the power of the erotic within our lives can give us the energy to pursue genuine change within our world, rather than merely settling for a shift of characters in the same weary drama.'[20]

Exploring the connection between sexuality and spirituality is not merely beneficial for encountering and becoming attentive to our embodiedness (although this is essential and powerful), it is also a powerful energy to change the world. I'll bet you didn't know that attending to the erotic in your life could be so significant and empowering!

Mindful masturbation: A spiritual practice

What kind of spiritual practice does this account of spirituality, sexuality and sexual pleasure lead us to? I want to suggest a practice of mindful masturbation as a spiritual practice. Mindfulness-based interventions in sexual practices such as masturbation have been demonstrated to improve trauma survivors' sexual satisfaction. Mindfulness allows such survivors to become and remain engaged during sex and to prevent the kind of body disassociation that can be commonplace. For those who are already experiencing a kind of embodied disassociation, mindful masturbation might also be a helpful technique in learning to encounter one's body as a safe space once again, in returning to our embodied being, and in dialling down unhelpful forms of hyper-vigilance. Attending to and noticing internal and external stimuli is associated with increased sexual satisfaction and positive sexual self-concept (the ways in which we understand ourselves as sexual persons). Learning to experience our bodies as places of pleasure, understanding ourselves positively as sexual beings, and recognizing that this sexual pleasure is not something to be subdued as sinful but revelled in as part of our spiritual lives is good for us!

Our bodies, bodily desires, passions and sexual impulses are not bad things. There are obvious limits around not hurting other people (without their consent) to be taken into account here, but I want to focus primarily on masturbation. Masturbating is a good thing. It enables a deep engagement with your bodily self that is rich, intimate and beneficial. It offers the opportunity to get to know ourselves better. Our sexuality is an expression of our spirituality.

So, here is your suggested practice:

- Masturbate.
- Pay attention to your body and your reactions to the ways in which you touch yourself. Be mindful of what is happening. Take it slow (or fast if you prefer!).
- Resist the phallocentric sexual scripts you've been given. Your whole body can experience pleasure. Take some time to touch other parts of yourself and find where you're sensitive (if you've ever watched Monica teach Joey and Chandler about the seven erogenous zones on *Friends* you'll know exactly what I mean).
- Recognize and be thankful for the capacity your body has to experience pleasure. This is a gift from God.
- Don't reach for orgasm. Just enjoy the sensations.
- Stop when you've had enough.
- Don't feel guilty.
- Make a date with yourself to do it again.

Moving on?

Don't. This is one of the practices in the book that is for all seasons. You don't need to move on from this. Be connected with your body. Recognize your sexual passions as a beautiful part of who you are and that sexual activities are not removed from spiritual things. Masturbation can be prayer too.

Notes

1 Heather Riggleman, 'Is Masturbation a Sin? What Does the Bible Say?', *Christianity.com*, 6 April 2022, https://www.christianity.com/wiki/sin/masturbation-a-sin.html, accessed 28.06.2024.
2 Vern L. Bullough, 'Masturbation', *Journal of Psychology & Human Sexuality* 14, no. 2–3 (23 January 2003), p. 19.
3 Jerome, *Against Jovinian*, 1.19.
4 John Calvin, 'Genesis Chapter 38', in *Commentary on Genesis*, trans. John King, Vol. 2 (Grand Rapids, MI: Christian Classics Ethereal Library), https://ccel.org/ccel/calvin/calcom02/calcom02.xvi.i.html, accessed 10.07.2024.
5 Brundage, 1987, p. 571 cited in Bullough, 'Masturbation', p. 26.
6 Malachi Willis et al., 'Are Women's Orgasms Hindered by Phallocentric Imperatives?', *Archives of Sexual Behavior* 47, no. 6 (1 August 2018), pp. 1565–76.
7 Willis et al., 'Are Women's Orgasms Hindered by Phallocentric Imperatives?'.
8 Willis et al., 'Are Women's Orgasms Hindered by Phallocentric Imperatives?'.
9 Hillary L. McBride, *The Wisdom of Your Body: Finding Healing, Wholeness, and Connection through Embodied Living* (Ada, MI: Brazos Press, 2021), p. 63.
10 McBride, *The Wisdom of Your Body*, p. 66.
11 Roxanne Guyon et al., 'Who Am I as a Sexual Being? The Role of Sexual Self-Concept Between Dispositional Mindfulness and Sexual Satisfaction among Child Sexual Abuse Survivors', *Journal of Interpersonal Violence* 38, no. 7–8 (1 April 2023), p. 5600.
12 Christine K. Hahn et al., 'Women's Perceived Likelihood to Engage in Sexual Risk Taking: Posttraumatic Stress Symptoms and Poor Behavioral Regulation', *Journal of Interpersonal Violence* 36, no. 11–12 (June 2021), p. 5872–83.
13 Joy R. Bostic, '"Flesh That Dances": A Theology of Sexuality and the Spirit in Toni Morrison's Beloved' in *The Embrace of Eros: Bodies,*

Desires and Sexuality in Christianity, ed. Margaret D. Kamitsuka (Minneapolis, MN: Fortress Press, 2010), p. 288.

14 For more detailed accounts of the place of Song of Songs in Christian spirituality see, for example, Andrew Louth, *Eros and Mysticism: Early Christian Interpretation of the Song of Songs* (London: Guild of Pastoral Psychology, 1992); Denys Turner, *Eros and Allegory: Medieval Exegesis of the Song of Songs*, Cistercian Studies Series 156 (Kalamazoo, MI: Cistercian Pubns, 1995); Mark S. Burrows, 'Allegorical Reading and Monastic Body-Building: Bernard of Clairvaux on the Song of Songs' in *Scrolls of Love. Essays on Ruth and the Song of Songs*, ed. Peter S. Hawkins and Lesleigh Cushing (New York: Fordham University Press, 2011).

15 Werner G. Jeanrond, *A Theology of Love* (London: A&C Black, 2010), p. 18.

16 Louise Nelstrop, 'Erotic and Nuptial Imagery', in *The Oxford Handbook of Mystical Theology*, ed. Edward Howells and Mark A. McIntosh (Oxford: Oxford University Press, 2020), pp. 336–7.

17 Hugh B. Urban, 'Sexuality' in *The Cambridge Handbook of Western Mysticism and Esotericism*, ed. Glenn Alexander Magee (Cambridge: Cambridge University Press, 2016), p. 429.

18 Urban, 'Sexuality', p. 430.

19 Audre Lorde, 'Uses of the Erotic: The Erotic as Power' in *Sister Outsider* (New York: The Crossing Press, 1984), p. 57.

20 Lorde, 'Uses of the Erotic', p. 59.

8

The Practice of Rest

I will both lie down and sleep, for you alone, O Lord, will keep me safe. (Ps. 4.8)

Come to me, all of you who are weary and carry heavy burdens, and I will give you rest. (Matt. 11.28)

There is something ironic about the fact that this chapter on rest was one of the hardest chapters to get written. Ironic because I was so busy I rarely found time to work on the research needed for this chapter. And ironic that it was only when forced to rest after surgery that I found what I wanted to say in this chapter and the time to sit quietly and write it.

Rest is hard. Which is why I do not think it is any surprise to see the huge range of books available on finding rest.[1] We are busy people living in a culture that requires more and more from us just to keep going. Working long hours, working second jobs, picking up the second or third shift when you get home, emotional labour, housework, childcare, elder care, life administration... the list goes on. We are busy people existing in a culture that promotes, rewards and expects busyness. It is hard to break free from the productivity urge! It is hard to find ways to wind down, relax, enjoy ourselves, to rest.

While some of the work already undertaken on rest is really helpful, I want to frame this exploration of rest, trauma and spirituality more specifically. In her book *Spirit and Trauma*, Shelly Rambo centres the motif of Holy Saturday at the heart of her trauma theology. The theology of Holy Saturday has since become integral to the work of trauma theology and found resonance in many other scholarly works on the subject.

Throughout all this, however, I think we have largely forgotten that Holy Saturday is a Sabbath day. In this chapter, I explore what it might mean for us as trauma survivors to remember that this powerful day of Holy Saturday, which has offered so much to our theologies, is also a Sabbath day.

Scripture and Holy Saturday

Holy Saturday is largely elided in the New Testament texts. Of course, in each Gospel the Sabbath day between the day of Jesus' death and the day of his resurrection does occur but it invites little commentary. In the Gospel of Mark, the author notes that, in the evening after Jesus' death and 'since it was the day of Preparation, that is, the day before the sabbath' (Mark 15.42), Jesus' body was wrapped in linen and laid in a tomb. 'When the sabbath was over' (Mark 16.1), the narrative picks up again with the visit of the women to the tomb to anoint Jesus' body. The Sabbath is, quite literally, absent from the narrative. The narrative in the Gospel of John is very similar, with the author reminding the reader that the Sabbath is a day of great solemnity (John 19.31) which is why the Jews did not want the crucified bodies to be left on crosses during the Sabbath. The Gospel according to Luke offers us slightly more to go on as the author adds in the line, 'On the sabbath they rested according to the commandment' (Luke 23.56b) between the burial in the tomb and the narration of the resurrection.

The Matthean author adds in to the space between the burial and the resurrection a curious little passage (Matt. 27.62–66) wherein the priests and Pharisees seem to be anxious that the disciples will not observe the Sabbath but will use the day of rest to undertake a heist to snatch Jesus' body! They remind Pilate of Jesus' claim that he would rise again after three days and ask that the tomb be guarded to prevent the disciples from faking a resurrection. Pilate agrees they can guard the tomb.

And that is it for the Gospels. All agree that the reason Jesus is laid in a tomb is that the Sabbath is approaching and something must be done with the body. Luke tells us that the disciples rested on the Sabbath day and Matthew tells us that some Jews were worried the disciples would *not* rest on this day.

There are, of course, some hints at the events of Holy Saturday in a couple of other places in the New Testament. In Paul's letter to the Ephesians, there is a curious little aside as Paul riffs on the word 'ascended', saying that using the word 'ascended' in reference to Jesus must also indicate a descent: 'What does it mean but that he had also descended into the lower parts of the earth?' (Eph. 4.9). This would seem to be an oblique reference to Jesus' descent into 'the lower parts of the earth' in between his death and resurrection.

Even more oblique is the reference in 1 Peter to the dead hearing the Good News: 'The gospel was proclaimed even to the dead...' (1 Pet. 4.6). Nothing more is said here but traditionally this sentence has been understood to refer to Jesus' descent into the place of the dead after his death and his declaring the gospel to them. It is from this text that the theological concept of the Harrowing of Hell has arisen in conjunction with theories of atonement such as *Christus Victor* which present Jesus as the victorious saviour who leads the righteous dead out of hell.

Theologies of Holy Saturday

Theologians in early Christianity knew of an account of Jesus' activity in hell between his death and his resurrection. Melito of Sardis, writing before the end of the second century, in a text often included in Catholic liturgy for Holy Saturday still today, writes of Jesus seeking out Adam and Eve to bring them out of hell and into the kingdom of heaven.[2] The idea was popular throughout the Middle Ages with the narrative being reproduced as entertainment in the form of dramas such as the 'Harrowing of Hell' found in the *Book of Cerne*.[3]

However, it is safe to say that, on its own, Holy Saturday had received little modern theological attention before the Swiss Catholic theologian Hans Urs von Balthasar wrote about it in the middle of the twentieth century. Balthasar became interested in this obscure theological day, largely elided from

Scripture and forgotten from theology, due to the visions of his friend and confidante Adrienne von Speyr. Speyr had converted to Catholicism and begun experiencing mystical visions, including that of Christ's descent into hell on Holy Saturday. These visions influenced Balthasar's own thinking and convictions on the topic which make an appearance in *Theo-Drama*, among other places in his writing. While this is a complex and rich theological argument, which I am not going to attempt to rehearse here, for our purposes it is most important to know that, for Balthasar, when Christ descends into hell, he is there as a dead man among the dead. Thus, in contrast to the theological ideas that had previously been articulated, Balthasar does not depict an active Christ in hell busily standing on his soap box and proclaiming the gospel to the dead, nor riding a white horse with banners lifted high as the dead triumphally follow him out of hell and into paradise. Christ is just dead, as everyone else in hell is dead. He is a dead man in hell.[4]

It is this powerful, challenging and complex work that is taken up by the trauma theologian Shelly Rambo in her book *Spirit and Trauma: A Theology of Remaining*. Rambo uses Balthasar as her primary dialogue partner in her construction of her theology of remaining which is her articulation of both the place in which trauma survivors find themselves in the aftermath of trauma, and her account of God's presence within that space.

Rambo draws on Balthasar's theology of Holy Saturday to resist the idea of a Harrowing of Hell. Jesus does not descend into hell victoriously; he is a dead man in Hell. For Rambo, as for Balthasar, Easter Sunday comes too early in our theology and our practice and makes Holy Saturday just a forerunner to the triumphal day of resurrection. She writes:

> The passage from death to life, as it is narrated in the crucifixion and resurrection accounts in Christianity, is more complex if viewed through the lens of trauma. There is no smooth passage from death to life. The narrative of Holy Saturday and the descent into hell provides a picture of what persists between death and life. The rhetoric of descent into hell ...

is not unlike a trauma narrative; the language of death, forsakenness, abandonment, and hopelessness is present. The middle day provides a fitting landscape to speak about the razed terrain of trauma.[5]

Rambo uses this space of Holy Saturday as a way of talking about the experience of the trauma survivor who exists in the aftermath of trauma – death, forsakenness, abandonment, hopelessness – and for whom there is not yet the triumphal victory of resurrection on Easter Sunday. She cautions preachers and teachers to resist rushing to the resurrection and glossing over the more complex experiences trauma survivors may have. She notes:

> One of the things I have been countering, in looking through the lens of trauma, is the tendency to rush to the proclamations of Easter and to its claims of new life and resurrection. In many Christian traditions, the movement from passion to resurrection, enacted liturgically, is seamless. Death is behind, and new life comes. Cornel West reveals the problematic dimensions of this approach. Speaking within the tradition of prophetic Christianity, he points to Holy Saturday as the day that most American Christian churches want to ignore. They want victory and good news, he says. The proclamation of Saturday, 'God is death,' stops us in our tracks by reminding us that victory does not come quickly, if it comes at all. Smoothing over this day is tied to a larger smoothing over of oppression, violence, and the injustices of history.[6]

The eliding of Holy Saturday liturgically and theologically is, in this reading, not a neutral error but part of a larger desire within our culture to avoid recognizing violence, abuse, injustice and oppression. When our focus is on victory and goodness, we spiritually bypass the realities of injustice, violence and oppression and leave trauma survivors with no acknowledgement of the reality of their experience and no spiritual space in which to exist in their trauma. It is a form of cultural and even ecclesial forsakenness.

Despite the forsakenness that Jesus experiences on Holy Saturday – which is interpreted 'redemptively as the complete solidarity of God with humanity'[7] – the Holy Spirit witnesses in this middle space to what persists between death and life. Rambo frames this remaining, middle Spirit as a thin, weary, trickle of Love that is, nonetheless, present, remaining, persisting and witnessing.

In this theology of Holy Saturday, space is found within the central narrative of the Christian story for the experience of trauma survivors and the solidarity of God as the Holy Spirit who remains always.

'I will both lie down and sleep in peace...'[8]

We have, then, in our exploration of Holy Saturday, both scripturally and theologically, a reminder that this space, which is so rich and helpful in theologically engaging in trauma and with trauma survivors, is a space of Sabbath rest. While there are many forms of rest, and the Sabbath is largely focused on not undertaking activity on a day that is supposed to be kept holy, I want to turn our attention to the ultimate form of rest – sleep.

Understanding sleep from a biblical and theological perspective is not simple. We might take the declaration in Psalm 4, 'I will both lie down and sleep in peace, for you alone, O Lord, make me lie down in safety', on its own and claim that God is keen on sleep as God protects us while we doze, but the truth is far more complex.

There *are* many positive descriptions and encounters with sleep in the Bible. In the Hebrew Bible, sleep is often a place where God is active. In the second chapter of Genesis, it is in Adam's deep sleep that Eve is created. Sleep is a divine gift rooted in the creation narrative where sleeping and waking are given by God. Abram (Gen. 15.12–16), Jacob (Gen. 28.10–17) and Job (Job 4.12–21) all experience deep sleep as places of revelation. And conversely, the lack of sleep is seen as a sign of suffering (Dan. 2, 6; Esth. 6). Sleep gets little positive mention in the New Testament (but plenty of negative attention – see below); but in Acts 12, Peter's sleep while in prison might be construed as a sign of his faith and trust in God.

But the Bible is also replete with imagery and narrative that depicts sleep as something dangerous and to be avoided. Sleep is often a dangerous time in which sleepers are vulnerable to physical and spiritual attacks. For example, in Judges 4 Jael stays awake (and is blessed) in order to kill Sisera who sleeps. On a different note – but still equally negative – the book of Proverbs depicts sleep as a time in which the individual is not engaged in action and therefore is associated with laziness and poverty (Prov. 6.11, 23.20–21).

This is all exacerbated by the sense that God does not sleep. In Psalm 121, the psalmist claims that God never sleeps. In fact, sleeping gods are neglectful gods (see 1 Kings 18). The psalmist contradicts the claim that God never sleeps, with frequent pleas that God would wake up (Ps. 7, 44.23, 59). The only time it is noted in the NT that Jesus is sleeping is when he is on the boat during a storm – note again that a sleeping God would seem to be a neglectful one! The disciples are chastised three times in the Garden of Gethsemane for falling asleep when they had been asked to stay awake and pray with Jesus (Matt. 8.23–27). While the contradiction is unhelpful, it seems clear that God does not (or at least *should* not) sleep and that sleeping is evidence of a lack of vigilance, which allows evil to occur. Sleep is not a neutral activity in the Scriptures; in fact, it would be difficult to claim that the Scriptures give any strong endorsement for sleeping.

But we must balance this scriptural claim with medical and psychological advice. Adults are recommended to get between seven and nine hours' sleep per night. Research has demonstrated that poor sleep correlates with long-term illnesses and that sleep deprivation results in psychosocial problems, increased stress and somatic issues. Recent research has indicated that sleep is luxury. John Groeger and Piril Hepsomali's wide-ranging survey of sleep in the UK revealed class, socio-economic and ethnic dimensions: 'The Problematic Sleep Index showed being younger, male, employed, home-owning, having a higher household income, having a higher level of educational achievement, and time in education were all associated with better sleep, as was living in a more affluent area and being White.'[9] They conclude:

> Sleep problems in Britain show a social gradient ... suggesting that sleep quality differs in and between different ethnic groups. These sleep inequalities suggest that the protective and recuperative effects of sleep are disproportionality distributed across society and should encourage us to consider the potential benefits of community-specific sleep interventions.[10]

Sleep is not neutral. Good quality sleep is a luxury enjoyed by people with more privilege in our society. The invention of electricity and the move towards 24-hour productivity has eroded both the importance of sleep and also the capacity to sleep. Thanks to both capitalism and the Protestant work ethic, work and productivity have a holy status. Sociologist Max Weber argues that in the Protestant work ethic, only action (that is, work and productivity) serves to increase God's glory.[11] Rest is articulated only in relation to work. The insistence on productivity as central to what it means to be human erodes the place of rest, which only then has value when it is setting you up for more work.

From a gendered perspective, sleep, rest, and the lack thereof play into long-entrenched gender binaries wherein activity is associated with the masculine, and passivity with the feminine. Men are active and embrace a manly wakefulness. Women are thus associated with passivity and sleep, which is ironic given that Groeger and Hepsomali's research indicate that it is men who are most likely to get good sleep. For women, sleep is often interrupted by their roles as caretakers.

To insist on sleep, therefore, is to resist capitalism, to resist the patriarchy, to resist racism, to insist on class equality, and to resist demands for economic productivity. Sleep is the ultimate form of resistance because it cannot be exploited. If sleep is liberative, then we might imagine sleeping to be in line with God's liberative actions. We might then have to parse our way through the scriptural accounts and agree that God does not sleep but that does not mean that we should not sleep. We can experience sleep as a place where God is active and where we might encounter God just as Abram, Jacob and Job did.

Reimagining Holy Saturday as a day of rest

What does all of this mean for us as we think through spiritual practices that might be of benefit to trauma survivors? As I outlined above, Holy Saturday has been a rich motif through which to imagine the space in which the trauma survivor exists, a space in which death and life are mingled, in which there is not yet any resolution; Holy Saturday is the place where the unimaginable has happened and there is not yet any victory, only the weary trickle of Love that always remains with us.

I want us to go a step further, though, and consider what it means to understand Holy Saturday as a Sabbath day. The Gospel of Luke indicates that, after the group of Jesus' friends and family had placed Jesus' body in the tomb, 'They rested according to the commandment', because it was the Sabbath. So what does Holy Saturday look like for this group of family, friends and disciples? The commandment of their faith tells them to rest. We might imagine, therefore, that they spend this time together in someone's home, grieving together. There's no activity on this day. We might imagine that they are in shock, that some of them are traumatized by witnessing the death of their friend or relation in such a brutal way.[12] They weep together, express their grief, pick at a meal perhaps? Had someone prepared a Sabbath meal in advance of the crucifixion? Did they bless God and praise Him as they would do normally on a Sabbath? We do not know, but we do know that they rested. They waited until the Sabbath was over before gathering their fragrant spices and walking back to the tomb to anoint the body of their loved one. After they had rested.

But what about Jesus? Jesus who, after his death, descended into hell? Jesus, who had celebrated many Sabbath meals with his family and his friends, opening tables to those who were never supposed to eat with him, the unclean, the unwanted, the unloved? I want us to imagine that even in his descent to the 'lower places of the earth' Jesus observes the Sabbath. Throughout his life, death and resurrection, Jesus is as much of a Jewish man as he is the second Person of the Trinity, so it should not be too much of a stretch of our imagination to think he might continue to observe the commandment from God to keep the Sabbath. This means, I suggest, that Jesus does not engage in any activity in his descent to hell. He rests. He does not preach to those who have died who were righteous, he is not riding a white horse, banners raised in preparation for a triumphal ascent. He rests as the commandment indicates he should. Considering the impact this idea might have upon atonement theories and divine passivity is work for another book, but thinking about what it means to follow Jesus is work for now. What does it mean to follow Jesus into this Holy Saturday space as trauma survivors? It means we can rest.

Rest as a spiritual practice

It is OK to rest. Our world does not make us feel like it, but it is OK to rest.

Try an experiment with me. Take a week and make it your mission to prioritize your rest. Whenever you are faced with a choice of activities, choose rest. Now that might mean that laundry does not happen for a week. It might mean eating very simple meals, eating out of the freezer. It might mean going to bed early, staying in bed longer in the morning. It might mean not showering every day. None of this will be the end of the world for a week.

What do you do with your rest? You do not have to do anything with it. You might watch some TV, you might read a favourite book, you might listen to some music. But you do not have to. You can lie on your bed and stare at the ceiling if you want to! You can sleep. You can just sleep. You do not have to be productive in your rest.

After the week is up, assess how it went. Where and when was it that you really felt able to rest? When did your body lose some its tension? When did your mind stop churning through all the activity and anxiety that you hold in your body? Whatever this resting place was, make it yours regularly moving forward. Try not to see this resting place as another task on your list but as a genuine opportunity to rest. It might be something you can do daily, or perhaps weekly. But whatever it is, prioritize resting.

A Prayer for the Resters

> Loving God, you whisper to us 'Rest, my beloved.'
> Let us hear the sweet invitation to rest with you.
> Spirit, hold us in your gentle arms and hum lullabies to us.
> Let each breath we take be full of your peace which passes all understanding.
> Give us the courage to rest, that we might be still and know you better. Amen.
>
> **Inhale:** I will lie down and sleep in peace.
> **Exhale:** For you alone, O Lord, make me dwell in safety.

Notes

1 See, for example, the following selection: Claudia Hammond, *The Art of Rest: How to Find Respite in the Modern Age* (Edinburgh: Canongate Books, 2019); Tricia Hersey, *Rest Is Resistance: Free Yourself from Grind Culture and Reclaim Your Life* (London: Hachette UK, 2022); Tricia Hersey, *Nap Ministry's Rest Deck* (San Francisco, CA: Chronicle Books, 2023); Adam Mabry, *The Art of Rest: Faith to Hit Pause in a World That Never Stops* (London: The Good Book Company, 2018); Mita Mistry, *All You Need Is Rest: Refresh Your Well-Being with the Power of Rest and Sleep* (London: Hachette UK, 2023); Ottessa Moshfegh, *My Year of Rest and Relaxation* (London: Random House, 2018); Alex Soojung-Kim Pang, *Rest: Why You Get More Done When You Work Less* (London: Penguin UK, 2016); Octavia F. Raheem, *Pause, Rest, Be: Stillness Practices for Courage in Times of Change* (Boulder, CO: Shambhala Publications, 2022); Nicola Slee, *Sabbath: The Hidden Heartbeat of Our Lives* (London: Darton, Longman & Todd, 2019).

2 Melito of Sardis, 'The Lord's Descent into Hell' in *A Homily for Holy Saturday* (The Vatican, n.d.), https://www.vatican.va/spirit/documents/spirit_20010414_omelia-sabato-santo_en.html, accessed 28.06.2024.

3 Anon., 'Book of Cerne' (Mercia; Cerne Abbey, Dorset, 9th century), Cambridge University Library.

4 This brief summary is based on the argument in Hans Urs von Balthasar, *Mysterium Paschale: The Mystery of Easter*, trans. A. Nichols (San Francisco, CA: Ignatius Press, 1970). Translated edition published in 2005.

5 Shelly Rambo, *Spirit and Trauma : A Theology of Remaining* (Louisville, KY: Westminster John Knox Press, 2010), p. 113.

6 Rambo, *Spirit and Trauma*, p. 129.

7 Rambo, *Spirit and Trauma*, p. 68.

8 I am heavily indebted to the superb work of a former student for this section. Revd Angela Tarry produced an outstanding MA thesis on sleep as a spiritual practice and I learned so much from supervising and engaging with this work with her. Thank you, Angela!

9 J. A. Groeger and P. Hepsomali, 'Social Deprivation and Ethnicity Are Associated with More Problematic Sleep in Middle-Aged and Older Adults', *Clocks and Sleep* 5, no. 3 (7 August 2023), p. 399.

10 Groeger and Hepsomali, 'Social Deprivation and Ethnicity', p. 399.

11 Max Weber, *The Protestant Ethic and the 'Spirit' of Capitalism: and other writings* (Penguin, 2002).

12 I have written about the idea that some of those at the foot of the cross might be traumatized by what they have experienced here: Karen O'Donnell, 'Surviving Trauma at the Foot of the Cross' in *When Did We See You Naked? Jesus as a Victim of Sexual Abuse*, ed. Jayme R. Reaves, David Tombs and Rocío Figueroa (London: SCM Press, 2021), pp. 260–77.

9

The Practice of Eating Good Food

Jesus said to them, 'Come and have breakfast.' (John 21.12a)

I really love food. I like eating it. I like cooking it. I like looking at recipes. I like watching videos of people making food, and videos of people sampling food in different cultures. I will watch pretty much any cooking show. I like to host people and cook them food. But I also have a pretty difficult relationship with food at times. When I am feeling down, cooking well for myself is one of the first things to go. The year I lived on my own, doing a job I hated, was the year I mainly ate toast and marmalade and Jaffa cakes for dinner.

Many of us have similarly ambivalent relationships with food and eating which makes writing a chapter like this a bit of a risk. If you do not think you are in a good place to think about food right now, then maybe skip this one and come back to it when you are feeling more positive about your relationship with food. In this chapter, I explore some of the ways in which the Christian tradition has encountered food in its Scriptures, its rituals, and in its spiritual practices. At the end of the chapter, I offer a spiritual practice of eating food you enjoy with people you love, in direct contrast to the more common spiritual practice of fasting alone. I want to allow space for a meal to remake us, bite by bite.

Food and eating in the Bible

Human relationship with God is entirely entwined with food. I always like to point out to my students in my 'Introduction to Christian Worship' class that if we consider characteristics and

THE PRACTICE OF EATING GOOD FOOD

accounts of worship throughout Scripture, we find so much is connected to food. In the Hebrew Scriptures, the Genesis narrative indicates that Yahweh had provided good food for humans and animals and that this was a blessing from God.

> God said, 'See, I have given you every plant yielding seed that is upon the face of all the earth, and every tree with seed in its fruit; you shall have them for food. And to every beast of the earth, and to every bird of the air, and to everything that creeps on the earth, everything that has the breath of life, I have given every green plant for food.' And it was so. (Gen. 1.29–30)

Many of the Hebrew days of celebration were connected to food. These were (and still are) literally called 'feast days' – days for feasting! The feast of Unleavened Bread (*Chag HaMatztot*), the feast of Weeks (*Shauvot*), and the feast of Booths (*Sukkot*) are all feasts connected to food and interwoven with the agricultural seasons – celebrating the first fruits of the grain and the collecting in of the harvest. Food is provided by God – whether in a successful harvest, in the creation narrative, or as manna and quail from heaven – and as such it is sacred. The psalmist writes 'He provides food for those who fear him; he is ever mindful of his covenant' (Ps. 111.5).

These are the practices into which Jesus was born and brought up, celebrating these feasts, eating these meals in his community and remembering the ways in which God had remembered his promises and provided food for his people. And so perhaps it is no surprise that, when asked by his followers how they should pray, Jesus tells them to ask God for their daily bread (Matt. 6.11). In the present day, we often allegorize this request to mean more abstract things such as 'Give us all we need to get through the day, strength, patience, resilience, wisdom ...', which is no bad thing to do. However, such a reading elides the pragmatic and traditional perspective of recognizing that all our food comes from God because he has promised it to us. It is harder to see that when I have walked around the supermarket with a list, contemplating the meals I need to make for my family in the coming week. *I have provided this food, courtesy of the supermarket and, if I am feeling particularly reflective, the farming and transportation industries that made this possible.* We have forgotten that food is sacred. It comes from God.

Jesus likes to eat. Robert Karris says, 'In Luke's Gospel Jesus is either going to meal, at a meal, or coming from a meal.'[1] This happens so much that Jesus' enemies accuse him of being a 'glutton and drunkard'. Imagine what those meals must have been like for that accusation to be made! Our images of Jesus are often of the emaciated figure on the cross. The Jesus whose ribs protrude through his skin, where every sinew of his frame is visible as his body is wrought in pain. But this is the same Jesus who is accused of being a glutton and a drunkard. The same Jesus who loves his food, loves to eat with his friends, loves to feed people, and makes the most important point about his ministry through a meal. This is no emaciated figure. What if Jesus was fat!?

This is the question Lisa Isherwood poses in her provocative text *The Fat Jesus*. Here she presents the figure of the 'corpulent Christ' – a fat Jesus who offers an incarnational invitation at the eucharistic table; a radical space of sensuous engagement and commitment.[2] Isherwood challenges the dominant discourses, both secular and Christian, of dieting and thinness, especially concerning the female body. She argues that 'fat' is no longer a symbol of strength and energy but is now a sign of social shame and a signal of a lack of control.[3] This religion of thinness has made us despise our bodies and has driven a wedge into our sense of wholeness, reinforcing a mind/body dualism that brings with it toxicity and damage. This battle against fat flesh is a battle against nature itself. The fat body, the message rings clear, is not a spiritual body. It is a sinful body – one out of control that must be conquered. The appetites must be suppressed. The desires of this body are sinful.

Distrust of appetite

Suspicion and mistrust of one's appetite is not a new thing, it is not even a Christian thing. It is, famously, Socrates' description of what the (hu)man is like. In *Phaedrus*, a text written by Plato 'recalling' the teachings of his mentor Socrates, Socrates likens the person to a chariot driven by two horses. One horse is beautiful and noble and is our finer spirit. The other horse is ugly and bad! It is our base nature, driven by passions, appetites and irrationality. Our soul is the driver of this chariot and is trying to keep control of the horses, who are pulling in different directions. The soul – the truest sense of one's self – is trying to pull the appetites into line.

This dualistic way of understanding the body has a long legacy in Christian thought, as we have already seen in this book. Bringing the body under the control of the more rational, more trustworthy mind/soul has been a recurring theme. This is never more true than when we talk about bodies and appetite for food. There is a heritage in Christianity of producing weight loss programmes that specifically connect fat with sin and disobedience to God. Isherwood notes that 'the old binaries are in place in the Christian diet industry and they carry with them the hierarchical realities'.[4] The hierarchy is clear. Soul trumps body. And bodily appetites cannot be trusted.

Jesus points out that you can't win!

> For John the Baptist has come eating no bread and drinking no wine, and you say, 'He has a demon'; the Son of Man has come eating and drinking, and you say, 'Look, a glutton and a drunkard, a friend of tax-collectors and sinners!' (Luke 7.33–34)

Fasting and the (female) mystics

Fasting has long been associated with the spiritual life. Jesus fasted, not only during his 40 days in the desert after his baptism, but at other times in his life as well. As a Jew, he probably fasted prior to or during certain religious festivals. But Jesus instructs his followers about fasting in a way that suggests fasting, in Jesus' lifetime, was probably a more regular devotional practice. The author of the Gospel of Matthew writes that Jesus says:

> And whenever you fast, do not look somber, like the hypocrites, for they mark their faces to show others that they are fasting. Truly I tell you, they have received their reward. But when you fast, put oil on your head and wash your face, so that your fasting may be seen not by others but by your Father who is in secret; and your Father who sees in secret will reward you. (Matt. 6.16–18)

Fasting is clearly a normal practice in Jesus' own time, although with some less than holy practices caught up around it that Jesus wants, in this passage at least, to condemn. Throughout the centuries, fasting has been a common practice in various modes of spiritual life, not confined to Christianity. 'The spiritual act of fasting in archaic societies manifests itself in a series of mystical practices – the confession of sins, prayer, reclusion, humiliation, contrition, isolation which were always associated with abstinence from food.'[5] Voluntary hunger was a required practice for Christians and by the early Middle Ages this manifested itself as three fasting days a week. With the commonplace nature of this practice in mind, it is not really fasting that I am focusing on in this chapter, but rather eating.

A notable insertion into the history of fasting, worthy of spending a little time assessing, is the ways in which food – both eating it and not eating it – featured particularly in the lives of medieval women mystics. This has been thoroughly explored in various works by the notable scholar of Christian history Caroline Walker Bynum (to whom I am very much indebted for this analysis). Bynum writes:

> When medieval writers spoke of eating or tasting or savoring God, they meant not merely to draw an analogy to a particular bodily pleasure but, rather, to denote directly an experience, a feeling/knowing of God into which the entire

THE PRACTICE OF EATING GOOD FOOD

person was caught up. The mystical writer Rudolph Biberach (d. ca. 1350) pointed out that *sapientia* (wisdom, good taste) and *sapere* (to taste or savor) are related etymologically: 'to taste' is 'to know' ... Thus almost all medieval mystics sometimes speak of 'tasting God'.[6]

If you want to think about eating food (or the lack thereof) and the spiritual life, there's no better place to turn to than some of the women mystics of the medieval period. With particular focus on the Eucharist (but not exclusively so), many of these women mystics not only utilized language of hungering, devouring, savouring and tasting as part of their spiritual vocabulary, but also experienced eating and drinking as part of their mystical experiences. Bynum notes:

> Women's ways of serving their fellow Christians and of uniting with God were closely tied to food, both symbolically and in fact. Medieval women fed others. They abstained in order to feed others. They fed others with their own bodies, which, as milk or oil, became food. They ate or drank the suffering of their fellow creatures by putting their mouths to putrifying sores. Moreover, women achieved ecstatic union by fusing with a God who became food on the altar. In a fierce imitation of the cross that included self-flagellation, self-starvation, and acute illness, women became the macerated body of the Savior, the bleeding meat they often saw in eucharistic visions. In erotic union with the adorable body of Jesus, they felt grace within as inebriating drink or as a melting honeycomb.[7]

The narratives of medieval woman mystics, particularly those in the Low Countries that Bynum focuses on, are replete with accounts of fasting, of eating only the Eucharist, and of experiencing the reception of the Eucharist as a mystical encounter with God (or vice versa, where a vision experience often entailed being given Jesus' own body to eat, feeding at his breasts, or receiving the Eucharist from his own hand).

One of my favourite mystics in this genre is Hadewijch, who was a thirteenth-century mystic probably living in the Duchy of

Brabant (now the Netherlands). She was, for a time, the head of a house of Beguines – a lay order of Christian women, particularly active in the Low Countries in the thirteenth to sixteenth centuries. Hadewijch longed to experience union with Christ and encouraged her fellow women to 'be God with God'.[8] This union is, for Hadewijch, best understood through hunger and eating: '*To hunger* and *to devour*, for her, had clear overtones of physicality joining physicality. *To eat* meant both to fuse with, in erotic union of mouth to mouth, and to become pregnant with, to have grown within one's belly.'[9] Hadewijch is clear that, through the Eucharist, we do eat God:

> ... love's most intimate union
> Is through eating, tasting and seeing interiorly.
> He eats us; we think we eat him,
> And we do eat him, of this we can be certain.[10]

Not only do we eat God in the Eucharist, but we are also, for Hadewijch, eaten by God. She is expressing a sense of interpenetration, an intermingling of physicality, of self, of humanity, in this experience of the Eucharist. Indeed, in some of her writings, there is a clear erotic charge to her encounters with God.

> After that [receiving the Eucharist from God] he came himself to me, took me entirely in his arms, and pressed me to him; and all my members felt his in full felicity, in accordance with the desire of my heart and my humanity. So I was outwardly satisfied and fully transported.[11]

Hadewijch experiences an orgasm as God presses himself to her after giving her food from his body in the Eucharist.

Hadewijch is just one example of the many women in the medieval period who experienced mystical encounters with God that were entwined with food. Bynum argues that this is partly because food was one of the few commodities medieval women had any control over and that, in some cases, these foody mystical experiences were ways of circumventing ecclesial authority (for example, when one was given the Eucharist from the hand of Christ himself, after being denied or restricted access to the Eucharist by the priest). But whatever the reasons, it is clear that food, eating, hungering, devouring, feasting, fasting – all are entwined with the spiritual life.

Trauma and food

Many of us who are trauma survivors have complicated relationships with food. A number of research projects have examined this complicated relationship and indicate that exposure to traumatic events has been associated with later eating disorder symptoms.[12] Sexual forms of trauma are more likely to correlate with anorexia, whereas most other forms of trauma are more likely to correlate with binge eating disorders.[13] The research has made clear that trauma 'has a negative impact on personal resources such as social interactions and one's sense of coherence'.[14] We know that trauma impacts on the ways in which we perceive our bodies, and can isolate us from our important relationships. It is perhaps unsurprising then that the embodied experience of trauma has an embodied impact on our eating. When we do not see ourselves clearly, when we do not love ourselves or find ourselves worthy of love, and when we shut down the relationships that would have shared food with us, it is no wonder we might struggle to eat properly.

I am not a medical expert or a nutritionist. As we move into this reconstructive section that might offer some insight into how eating food could be a spiritual practice, if you are someone who has this kind of complicated relationship with food, it might be a good idea to talk to your doctor about it and ensure that a holistic approach to this practice is taken. I strongly believe that eating good food well with others can be a radical, subversive and powerful spiritual act. But in order to be so, it needs to not cause us pain and suffering any further in our bodies. Be careful. Be kind to yourself.

The experiential pleasure of food

In a 2019 piece of research, Wided Batat et al. set out to challenge the idea of eating food as a guilty pleasure and its association with a form of moral failure.[15] They articulate what they name as the Experiential Pleasure of Food: the 'enduring cognitive (satisfaction) and emotional (i.e. delight) value consumers gain from savoring the multisensory, communal, and cultural meaning in food experiences'.[16] This includes both the immediate food experience as well as the remembering and the anticipation of food. The research team break this down into three stages: the contemplation stage, the connection stage, and the creation stage.

In the contemplation stage of this experiential pleasure, the team highlight the significance of the multisensory nature of pleasurable food experiences and the emotional reactions we might have to such experiences. They point to the significance of the visual aesthetics of a plate of food and even surmise that pausing to Instagram photos of one's food might actually increase savouring behaviour. We are food-sensory beings who can take pleasure in thinking about what we are going to eat.[17]

The second stage of this experiential pleasure of food is the connection stage in which we recognize the sociocultural nature of food and the significance of food sharing. Batat et al. note, 'Foods and their consumption are part of the cultural material that repeatedly constructs one's cultural identity.'[18] After all, we are what we eat! Sharing food reinforces values and norms and strengthens community ties. The practice of eating together is essential to family identity and unity. Ultimately, eating together makes us healthier in both body and mind.[19]

The third stage of this food journey is the creation stage in which symbolism and storytelling are emphasized. Food offers the means for understanding. The symbolism of food and food practices reinforces shared cultural, social and religious identities. One only has to think of the Eucharist in Christianity, or the langar kitchen in Sikhism, or the turkey on the Thanksgiving table in the United States. Food storytelling is a memory-laden activity. Such eating plays with time as meaning from the past is drawn into the present eating experience, with anticipation of future eating experiences.[20]

Already the relationship between this way of understanding food and the practice of post-traumatic remaking that we outlined at the very beginning of this book is becoming clear. In our practice of post-traumatic remaking we are seeking ways of telling our story of trauma and understanding what has happened to us in a broader context of meaning. We are looking to attend to the body and not dissociate it from the mind. We are looking for practices that might begin to reconnect us to our communities (or help us to find new communities). These imperatives for post-traumatic remaking are mirrored beautifully in this account of the experiential pleasure of food. Each of the stages outlined gives space for attending to the body, from literally savouring the sensory pleasures of food to facilitating emotional responses to the food that are grounded in both individual and sociocultural contextual encounters with food. Meaning-making and memory, telling stories, grounding in symbolism, giving space for new encounters while remembering those that have gone before – all these activities are entwined with the eating of food in this way. Learning who we are and building connections with those around us are at the heart of this pleasure in food.

Our spiritual practice: Eat good food well with others

I think you can probably already tell what our spiritual practice is going to be with this chapter! It's a relatively simple one in that it involves something we do every day – eating – but, as we have seen throughout this chapter, there's nothing really very simple about food at all. At its heart, my suggestion for a spiritual practice of remaking is to eat food you enjoy with others. This might be pizza with friends, a Sunday lunch with family, coffee and cake with a loved one, a fancy ten-course tasting menu with your lover ... the specifics of the food do not actually matter. What does matter is that it is food you enjoy, that you eat it with people you love, and that you focus on the food (so I don't suggest, for example, something in front of the TV or popcorn at the cinema). There is an intentionality required in this practice and I suggest you draw upon the three-stage journey of the experiential pleasure of food as you engage in this practice.

1. *The contemplative stage*

To begin with, anticipate this eating. You might be cooking it, which makes it easier to anticipate as you perhaps peruse cookbooks, source ingredients, begin cooking. If you're going out for the meal, perhaps you might take a look at the menu and anticipate what choices you'll make. Take some time before this particular eating experience to reflect on the food you like and why you like it, recognize what your body is telling you, consider what memories are evoked by dwelling in this anticipation. If you like to, take photos of your food when it is ready or it arrives before you. You can post these to Instagram if you like but enjoy the visual quality of the food and all the pleasure that brings to you.

Take a few moments to say a grace, a blessing on the food. You might do this on your own in your interior voice if it's not an appropriate place or group to pray such a prayer, but you might ask those with you to pray it as well. You may have your own favourite grace but the one I like to use is:

> Bless, O God, this food to our use and our lives to your service, and give us a hunger for justice until all are fed. Amen.[21]

2. *The connection stage*

You'll probably want to reflect on this after eating, depending on the nature of the meal, but take some time to appreciate the time together with those with whom you share this meal. The culinary essayist Jean Anthelme Brillat-Savarin says, 'Tell me what you eat, and I will tell you who you are.'[22] Take some time to think about what you have eaten and reflect on what that says about who you are. How does this meal, food you enjoy eaten with people you love, help to narrate something of yourself, the context of your trauma, and your relationship with God?

3. The creation stage

What does this meal symbolize to you? What stories surround it as you eat food you enjoy with people you love? Remembering that Jesus loved to eat and drink with his friends and that the primary command he left to those who followed him was to eat and to drink as they remembered him and told stories of his life, how does this meal fit into that (eucharistic) meal? Allow your reflections on your meal to grow big, take time to digest all that it symbolizes. What new stories might you be able to start to tell after the eating of this meal?

It might be useful to journal your thoughts and reflections related to this meal both as an appetizer to eating it and as a digestif to follow it. Plan another meal. Eat food you enjoy regularly with people you love and allow your body to feel all the benefits of such a practice. Thank God for the food, for the people, for the memories, for the stories, and for the anticipation of future meals.

Allow yourself to be remade, one bite at a time.

Notes

1 Robert J. Karris, *Eating Your Way Through Luke's Gospel* (Collegeville, MN: Liturgical Press, 2006), p. 14.
2 Lisa Isherwood, *The Fat Jesus: Feminist Explorations in Boundaries and Transgressions* (London: Darton, Longman & Todd, 2008), p. 31.
3 Isherwood, *The Fat Jesus*, p. 23.
4 Isherwood, *The Fat Jesus*, p. 31.
5 Cited in John Coveney, *Food, Morals and Meaning: The Pleasure and Anxiety of Eating*, 2nd ed. (London: Routledge, 2006), p. 31.

6 Caroline Walker Bynum, *Holy Feast and Holy Fast: The Religious Significance of Food to Medieval Women* (Berkeley, CA: University of California Press, 1988), p. 151.

7 Bynum, *Holy Feast and Holy Fast*, p. 114.

8 Hadewijch, *The Complete Works*, trans. Columba Hart, Classics of Western Spirituality (New York: Paulist Press, 1980), p. 61.

9 Bynum, *Holy Feast and Holy Fast*, p. 154.

10 Hadewijch, *The Complete Works*, p. 353. Poem 16 'Love's Seven Names'.

11 Hadewijch, pp. 350–2, Poem 15.

12 Alexandra D. Convertino, Leslie A. Morland and Aaron J. Blashill, 'Trauma Exposure and Eating Disorders: Results from a United States Nationally Representative Sample', *The International Journal of Eating Disorders* 55, no. 8 (2022), p. 1080.

13 Convertino, Morland and Blashill, 'Trauma Exposure and Eating Disorders', pp. 179–85.

14 Sefik Tagay et al., 'Eating Disorders, Trauma, PTSD, and Psychosocial Resources', *Eating Disorders* 22, no. 1 (2014), p. 34.

15 Wided Batat et al., 'The Experiential Pleasure of Food: A Savoring Journey to Food Well-Being', *Journal of Business Research* 100 (2019), pp. 392–9.

16 Batat et al., 'The Experiential Pleasure of Food', p. 393.

17 Batat et al., 'The Experiential Pleasure of Food', p. 395.

18 Batat et al., 'The Experiential Pleasure of Food', p. 395.

19 Batat et al., 'The Experiential Pleasure of Food', p. 396.

20 Batat et al., 'The Experiential Pleasure of Food', pp. 396–7.

21 Thanks to Revd Ruth Harley for this grace.

22 Jean Anthelme Brillat-Savarin, *The Physiology of Taste*, trans. Fayette Robinson (Mineola, NY: Dover Publications, 2019), p. 3.

Afterword

Keep On Surviving

When I initially conceived of this book, I imagined this final chapter would be focused on exploring what it might mean to move on from these practices when you were done with them. It was only in the actual writing of the work that I realized most of the themes and practices we have explored together are not necessarily things that need to be moved on from. As I have concluded at the ends of the chapters on anger and on unforgiveness, these might not be places you want to stay in for ever and I have suggested ways in which you might want to move in a different direction with these experiences. But the other practices need to be considered in a couple of different ways.

I think that practices of rest, eating good food, pleasure and deconstruction can happily be considered practices for life! I am confident that persisting in these as spiritual practices will be good for you – body and soul – and will consistently draw you closer to God.

But what about the other two practices? What about protest and hopelessness? These two are a little more complex. Protest as a lifelong practice might run the risk of burnout and crushing disappointments. This one should be handled with care and in conversation with people who love you. If it is bringing more harm than good, moving you away from a God who hears your cry, then it might be time to take pause and rest.

And hopelessness? I hope the way I have outlined hopelessness as a spiritual practice makes it clear that the kind of hopelessness I am talking about is not the kind that means we give up on everything and retreat away from the world. It is just the opposite. The kind of hopelessness I have offered is the kind that spurs us to action. The kind that recognizes you are the hands of God. As Teresa of Avila would remind us:

Christ has no body but yours,
No hands, no feet on earth but yours,
Yours are the eyes with which He looks compassion
    on this world,
Yours are the feet with which He walks to do good,
Yours are the hands with which he blesses all the world.
Yours are the hands, yours are the feet,
Yours are the eyes, you are His body.
Christ has no body now but yours,
Yours are the eyes with which he looks compassion
    on this world.
Christ has no body now on earth but yours.[1]

Everything for a season

It feels a little cliché to turn to Ecclesiastes 3 at the end of a book like this but I think it is a cliché for a reason – it is right.

> For everything there is a season, and a time for every matter under heaven:
> a time to be born, and a time to die;
> a time to plant, and a time to pluck up what is planted;
> a time to kill, and a time to heal;
> a time to break down, and time to build up;
> a time to weep, and a time to laugh;
> a time to mourn, and a time to dance;
> a time to throw away stones, and a time to gather stones together;
> a time to embrace, and a time to refrain from embracing;
> a time to seek, and a time to lose;
> a time to keep, and a time to throw away;
> a time to tear, and a time to sew;
> a time to keep silent, and a time to speak;
> a time to love, and a time to hate;
> a time for war, and a time for peace. (Eccles. 3.1–8)

AFTERWORD: KEEP ON SURVIVING

I see in this list all of our spiritual practices – mourning, breaking down, loving, speaking, peace, silence – they are all there. There is a time for everything. The truth of the aftermath of trauma is that remaking is a complex, messy, non-linear process. And it is a process that is likely ongoing for the rest of a trauma survivor's life. I hope this book might be a companion throughout that process, to be picked up at the time it is needed, and to inspire creativity in spiritual practice. I hope, in that respect, that it is liberative.

Post-traumatic remaking

In response to the question about what trauma survivors can actually do in order to aid their own post-traumatic remaking, I have sought to present a few starting points. I have selected some themes, engaged in some analysis, and offered some practices. I am well aware of the deficiencies and insufficiencies of what is offered in this book. I hope this might be a book that is useful to people who are trying to engage in the hard work of post-traumatic remaking. I hope it might remind them that they are not alone and also that the Christian spiritual tradition has things to offer that might help. I hope this could be a conversation opener within congregations who might want to consider what kind of support and spirituality is on offer within the church and how it meets (or does not meet) the needs of those who are trauma survivors.

A prayer for the trauma survivors who are doing the remaking

God who remains, draw us close to you.
God who remains, shelter us under your wings.
God who remains, give us courage to imagine a different way.
God who remains, give us strength to rebuild and remake.
God who remains, carry us when we are weary.
God who remains, speak to us your words of loving-kindness.
God who remains, let us remain in you. Amen.

Note

1 Attributed to Teresa of Avila, 'Christ Has No Body But Yours', *Catholic-Link* (blog), https://catholic-link.org/quotes/st-teresa-of-avila-quote-christ-has-no-body-but-yours/, accessed 10.07.2024.

Appendix

In the Sacred Pause – Liturgical Resources for Holy Saturday

In the academic year 2023/24, I taught a class called Theology and Trauma for the first time. It was an undergraduate class taught in the Cambridge Theological Federation and it was, as you might imagine, very popular! For the assessment of their learning, half of the students' mark was generated through a group project. One particular group chose the assignment which tasked them with creating a set of liturgical resources that were trauma-informed and trauma-oriented for use on Holy Saturday. The work they produced blew me away! I offer here only a small sample of their brilliant work in the form of two sample liturgies and a set of prayers inspired by things they read in preparation for the assignment. The students are all ordinands preparing for ordination in the Church of England and therefore have focused their liturgies on models of services common in that Church. The liturgies combine readily available resources from the Common Worship suite of texts, alongside some of their own writing.

Everything that follows is the work of Ian Henderson, Mary Kilikidi, Dan Krawczyk and Claire Brocklesby.

Sample Service 1

A Service Exploring the Silence, Waiting and Presence of Holy Saturday

This service aims to hold the grief of Good Friday, while also dwelling in the seemingly hopeless reality of Holy Saturday. This service intentionally draws attention away from the cross and violence of Good Friday. It is imagined that this service will be held in a church that has already stripped its altar on Maundy Thursday, and you are asked to consider that any visible crosses or crucifixes may be, for some, a symbol of ongoing violence.

The Gathering

We come from scattered lives to meet with God.
Let us recognize his presence with us.

Silence is kept.

As God's people we have gathered:
let us worship him together.

The Introduction

The leader may introduce the service. This is an opportunity to signpost where pastoral care support can be sought during or after the service.

The leader invites the people to confession.

APPENDIX: SAMPLE SERVICE I

Prayers of Penitence

Beloved community, as we abide in the solemnity of
Holy Saturday,
we may find ourselves in a place of profound uncertainty and
reflection, reminiscent of the disciples' vigil.
We are invited to pause and dwell in this liminal space, where
light has not yet pierced the shadow.
Let us confess our sins as an act of trust in the God who walks
with us through every darkness,
every moment of waiting, and every season of disorientation.

Pause for reflection

O God, who is ever-present in the midst of our deepest night,
we come before you in the stillness of this day, hearts heavy
and spirits sombre,
reflecting on the disciples' own bewilderment and sorrow on
that first Holy Saturday.

Pause for reflection

We confess, O Lord, that, like them, we too find ourselves
disoriented by life's trials,
daunted by the shadows that linger, and perplexed by the
silences where we expected your voice.

We admit our struggles, our quickness to despair,
and our slowness to remember your steadfast presence in
all things.

Pause for reflection

In your boundless mercy, meet us here in the depths of
our vulnerability.
Forgive us for our doubts, our fears, and the ways we fail to
trust in your abiding love.

SURVIVAL

Grant us the grace to endure this in-between, to find solace in the mystery,
and to hold space for our grief and confusion, knowing that you, O God, are with us in our waiting.

Give us the strength to embrace the discomfort of not knowing, and to find peace in the promise that you are God, even in the silence, even in the darkness.

Help us to bear witness to each other's journeys, to offer love where there is pain, and to extend grace where there is faltering.

In this sacred pause, renew our spirits and bind us together in the fellowship of shared uncertainty,
that we may support one another.

Amen.

Liturgy of the Word

Ecclesiastes 3.1–8
For everything there is a season, and a time for every matter under heaven:
a time to be born, and a time to die;
a time to plant, and a time to pluck up what is planted;
a time to kill, and a time to heal;
a time to break down, and a time to build up;
a time to weep, and a time to laugh;
a time to mourn, and a time to dance;
a time to throw away stones, and a time to gather stones together;
a time to embrace, and a time to refrain from embracing;
a time to seek, and a time to lose;
a time to keep, and a time to throw away;
a time to tear, and a time to sew;
a time to keep silent, and a time to speak;
a time to love, and a time to hate;
a time for war, and a time for peace.

APPENDIX: SAMPLE SERVICE 1

Luke 23.6–9
When Pilate heard this, he asked whether the man was a Galilean. And when he learned that he was under Herod's jurisdiction, he sent him off to Herod, who was himself in Jerusalem at that time. When Herod saw Jesus, he was very glad, for he had been wanting to see him for a long time, because he had heard about him and was hoping to see him perform some sign. He questioned him at some length, but Jesus gave him no answer.

Responding to the Word

Musicians: 'The Lord is My Light' (Taizé: *Complete Anglican Hymns Old & New* 944; *Psalms for All Seasons* 27A)

The musicians will sing 'The Lord is My Light' which is a hymn based on Psalm 27. We continue to hold an atmosphere of waiting as we dwell in the darkness of Holy Saturday. As we do that, we trust that God holds us in this space. In the darkness of Holy Saturday, we seek God's guidance and draw upon the promise that darkness is as light to Him.

The opportunity to light a votive candle

The congregation are invited to respond to this promise, if they choose, by coming forward to the bare altar to light a candle.

A period of silence

A period of silence is held.

The leader could remind people where pastoral support is located if needed during this time.

SURVIVAL

A poem

Stand still. The trees ahead and bushes beside you
Are not lost. Wherever you are is called Here,
And you must treat it as a powerful stranger,
Must ask permission to know it and be known.
The forest breathes. Listen. It answers,
I have made this place around you.
If you leave it, you may come back again, saying Here.
No two trees are the same to Raven.
No two branches are the same to Wren.
If what a tree or a bush does is lost on you,
You are surely lost. Stand still. The forest knows.
('Lost' by David Wagoner)

A pause for silence

Affirmation of Faith

You are invited to stand, if comfortable to do so, to affirm our faith together.

**I believe in the Father who shaped the silence of the universe,
in the Son who walked quietly among us,
and in the Spirit who whispers truth in moments of solitude.
This divine silence surrounds me, affirming God's presence in the quiet.**

Prayers

You are invited to find a position that is comfortable for you in prayer.

Almighty God, we find ourselves in a sacred pause.
We hold space for our grief, our uncertainties, and the deep
　yearnings of our hearts.

Grant us, O Lord, the grace to dwell here
   with faith and patience.
Teach us to listen for your still, small voice
   in the midst of our waiting,
reminding us that even in the darkest night,
your love and presence are unwavering.

Comfort all who carry the weight of trauma and loss,
enveloping them in your peace that surpasses understanding.
Strengthen our community, that we offer solace and support
   on journeys through the shadows.

As we reflect on the mystery of your love,
help us to feel your grace.
May this time draw us closer to you and to each other,
forging bonds of compassion and understanding.

We ask this in the name of Jesus Christ,
as we wait in the silence of the tomb.
Amen.

The Lord's Prayer

Lord, remember us in your kingdom
as we pray in the words you gave us:
**Our Father, who art in heaven,
hallowed be thy name;
thy kingdom come;
thy will be done;
on earth as it is in heaven.
Give us this day our daily bread.
And forgive us our trespasses,
as we forgive those who trespass against us.
And lead us not into temptation;
but deliver us from evil.
For thine is the kingdom,
the power and the glory
for ever and ever. Amen.**

Hymn

Hymn: 'Be Still and Know' (*Complete Anglican Hymns Old & New* 66; *Songs of Fellowship* 41)

Please feel free either to join in the hymn or to listen and reflect as appropriate.

Conclusion

We encourage you to leave this space in silence. However, know that the pastoral care team are at hand after the service if it should be helpful to talk or pray with someone else.

The leader says the final prayer.

As we depart from this sacred pause, may we carry with us the peace that comes from God's unwavering presence in our moments of waiting and darkness.
We go forth, bearing the light of hope that, even in silence, God weaves our stories of disorientation into his tapestry of grace.
Amen.

Sample Service 2

At the Tomb of Jesus

This service was designed to bring us into remembrance of the profound mystery encapsulated in the Passion, crucifixion and death of Jesus that took place yesterday. In the quiet, still ambience of the tomb, amid the realm of the unknown, we gather to offer our worship and present our 'final tribute' to Jesus, mirroring Mary Magdalene's act of tending to his holy body. Just as Mary did on the original Holy Saturday, we approach today bearing the weight of sorrow, yet anchored in the hope found in God's name and love.

We encourage the creation of a designated area within your church for a simple cross, bereft of Christ's figure, to stand. This may be accompanied by a white cloth or a modest candle at its base, serving as a symbol of Jesus' body resting in the tomb.

The Gathering

The leader says:

In the name of the Father,
and of the Son, and of the Holy Spirit.
Amen.

We come from scattered lives to meet with God.
Let us recognize his presence with us.

Silence is kept.

As God's people we have gathered:
let us worship him together.

The Penitence

The leader says:

Christ himself bore our sins in his body on the cross so that,
free from sin, we might live for righteousness;
by his wounds we have been healed.

Let us confess our sins.

**Almighty God, lover of all people, giver of all grace,
look mercifully upon us who acknowledge our sins;
create in us a pure heart and a steadfast spirit;
and lead us in the paths of holiness and righteousness;
through Jesus Christ our Lord.
Amen.**

The Liturgy of the Word

The reader introduces the Old Testament reading.
The first reading is taken from Lamentations 3.19–33.

The thought of my affliction and my homelessness
is wormwood and gall!
My soul continually thinks of it
and is bowed down within me.
But this I call to mind,
and therefore I have hope:

The steadfast love of the Lord never ceases,
his mercies never come to an end;
they are new every morning;
great is your faithfulness.
'The Lord is my portion,' says my soul,
'therefore I will hope in him.'

The Lord is good to those who wait for him,
to the soul that seeks him.

It is good that one should wait quietly
for the salvation of the Lord.
It is good for one to bear
the yoke in youth,
to sit alone in silence
when the Lord has imposed it,
to put one's mouth to the dust
(there may yet be hope),
to give one's cheek to the smiter,
and be filled with insults.

For the Lord will not
reject for ever.
Although he causes grief, he will have compassion
according to the abundance of his steadfast love;
for he does not willingly afflict
or grieve anyone.

At the end the reader says:
This is the word of the Lord.
Thanks be to God.

You might want to say together Psalm 22.

The reader introduces the Gospel reading.

Hear the Gospel of our Lord Jesus Christ according to John.
Glory to you, O Lord.

John 19.25–27
Meanwhile, standing near the cross of Jesus were his mother, and his mother's sister, Mary the wife of Clopas, and Mary Magdalene. When Jesus saw his mother and the disciple whom he loved standing beside her, he said to his mother, 'Woman, here is your son.' Then he said to the disciple, 'Here is your mother.' And from that hour the disciple took her into his own home.

At the end the reader says:

This is the Gospel of the Lord.
Praise to you, O Christ.

The Psalm and Canticle

In this sample service, you're invited to write and say your own Psalm of Lament.

After the Psalm is finished, we say together the Canticle:

Christ suffered for you, leaving you an example,
that you should follow in his steps.

He committed no sin, no guile was found on his lips,
when he was reviled, he did not revile in turn.

When he suffered, he did not threaten,
but he trusted himself to God who judges justly.

Christ himself bore our sins in his body on the tree,
that we might die to sin and live to righteousness.

By his wounds, you have been healed,
for you were straying like a sheep,
but have now returned
to the shepherd and guardian of your soul.

Glory to the Father,
and to the Son,
and to the Holy Spirit.
As it was in the beginning,
is now, and ever shall be:
world without end.
Amen.

APPENDIX: SAMPLE SERVICE 2

The Creed

The leader says:
We say together the Creed:

I believe in the Father, who hears our cries,
in Jesus Christ, who lamented over Jerusalem and cried out
in forsakenness,
and in the Holy Spirit, who intercedes for us with groans too
deep for words.
In my lament, I am joined to the suffering of Christ, finding in
my cries a sacred echo of his own,
a lament that is held and honoured by the Trinity, assuring me
that in my deepest pain,
I am not alone, but deeply connected to the heart of God.
Amen

The Prayers

The intercessor introduces prayers:
We bring our sorrows, our struggles, our doubts in the
presence of God and of each other,
on the day when the whole creation pauses to mourn the
death of the Saviour of the world.

About the dignity of creation that has been neglected, used,
hurt, and side-lined,
We lament.

About the peace lost, restoration that is not yet present, and
reconciliation that is still far away,
We lament.

About human indifference, greed and a deep sense of injustice,
We lament.

About human promises not being fulfilled, trust broken, hope abandoned,
We lament.

About those who have been hurt, silenced, not believed,
We lament.

About those who have been powerless and trapped in their circumstances,
We lament.

About those who have been wounded by society and by the Church,
We lament.

About those who have lost faith and lost hope,
We lament.

We bring our sorrows, our struggles, our doubts in the presence of God and of each other,
on the day when the whole creation pauses to mourn the death of the Saviour of the world.

**Merciful Father, accept our lamentations,
for the sake of your Son, our Saviour, Jesus Christ.
Amen.**

The Lord's Prayer

The leader begins the Lord's Prayer:

As we stand at the tomb, after the events of the Cross, let us pray as our Saviour has taught us:

**Our Father, who art in heaven,
hallowed be thy name;
thy kingdom come;**

thy will be done;
on earth as it is in heaven.
Give us this day our daily bread.
And forgive us our trespasses,
as we forgive those who trespass against us.
And lead us not into temptation;
but deliver us from evil.
For thine is the kingdom,
the power and the glory
for ever and ever.
Amen.

The Praise and Thanksgiving

The leader announces the hymn: (*Hymns Ancient & Modern* 523; *The New English Hymnal* 93)

We sing together 'Were you there when they crucified my Lord?'

The Conclusion

The leader says:

Gracious God,
as we conclude our time in your sacred pause,
grant us the courage to seek your presence in our lives
and the strength to offer your love to those around us.
May we be a beacon of your comfort and hope to all who navigate the shadows.
Amen.

Additional Material for 'In the Sacred Pause'

Sources used in developing the liturgies

Adam, David, *The Rhythm of Life – Celtic Daily Prayer* (London: SPCK, 2008).
Colquhoun, Frank, *New Parish Prayers*, New Edition (London: Hodder & Stoughton, 2005).
Joint Advisory Panel, *Celebrating Common Prayer – the Daily Office SSF* (Bristol: Mowbray, 1992).
The Archbishops' Council, *Common Worship*, all editions and volumes (London: Church House Publishing).
The Archbishops' Council, *New Patterns of Worship* (London: Church House Publishing, 2019).

Prayers Inspired by Writings on Trauma

This short set of prayers was written by the students in response to some of the reading they undertook while studying this course and preparing their resources. The first two are general prayers that might be used at any point in private or public worship. The third is to be included as an intercession and the fourth is to be used as a collect.

Prayer inspired by *What My Bones Know* by Stephanie Foo[1]

Gracious God, in the midst of pain there is a space for grace without the immediate rush to hope. In our journey through the wilderness of our souls, help us hold on to that grace, acknowledging our pain without being consumed by it. Guide us in the shape-shifting journey of healing, as we navigate the return of memories or the appearance of triggers, fighting each battle with your strength anew. May we find solace in your presence, the unchanging constant in our ever-changing struggle. Amen.

Prayer inspired by *Trauma-Sensitive Theology* by Jennifer Baldwin[2]

Healing Spirit, speak to the restoration of divine energy through life and relationships as the source of true salvation. As we navigate our lives, we ask for your soothing presence to heal and unburden the wounds and beliefs that may have been inflicted upon us. May our communities find unity in your compassionate wisdom, and may individuals feel reconnected to the loving awareness of their whole selves, reducing the felt separation from you and the global web of life. Amen.

Intercession inspired by *The Choice* by Edith Eger[3]

Lord of Liberation, teach us the power of choice in the aftermath of trauma – the choice to dismantle the prisons of our mind, brick by brick. Today, we pray for the strength to accept what is, to forgive ourselves, and to open our hearts to the miracles that exist now. In the sacred present, help us reclaim our inner truth, our strength, and our innocence. May we live now with the freedom of accepting your grace, finding peace in the acceptance of our reality. Amen.

Collect inspired by Tarry Awhile *by Selina Stone*[4]

Eternal Companion, illuminate the essential role of darkness in the journey of creation and life itself. In the quiet and absence of light this Holy Saturday, remind us that darkness is not devoid of your Spirit but is rather the prime space for your work within us. As we sit in silent prayer, transform us, overturning the harmful silences that have held us captive. In this day of darkness, may we find the courage to embrace the fertile ground from which new life springs. Come, Lord Jesus, and make your hidden work in us known. Amen.

Notes

1 Stephanie Foo, *What My Bones Know: A Memoir of Healing from Complex Trauma* (London: Atlantic Books, 2022).

2 Jennifer Baldwin, *Trauma-Sensitive Theology: Thinking Theologically in the Era of Trauma* (Eugene, OR: Cascade Books, an imprint of Wipf and Stock Publishers, 2018).

3 Edith Eva Eger and Esmé Schwall Weigand, *The Choice: Embrace the Possible* (London: Simon and Schuster, 2017).

4 Selina Stone, *Tarry Awhile: Wisdom from Black Spirituality for People of Faith: The Archbishop of Canterbury's Lent Book 2024* (London: SPCK, 2023).

Index of Names and Subjects

abandoned 55, 142
abandonment 62, 104
abolitionist 53
abortion 67
Abraham 69
Abram 105, 108
absence 13, 52–3, 146
abstinence 116
abuse 11, 14, 18, 22, 57, 68, 71, 81, 98, 104, 11
abuser 5, 11
acceptance 26, 54, 55, 142, 145
accuse, accusation 55, 61, 64, 114
activism 60–1, 69, 71
activist 33, 60
advocate 14, 59
affect 5, 22, 35
affective 28, 36, 64
affection 77
affliction 46, 50, 78, 138
Africa 64
African 19, 63, 72, 96
aftermath 1, 8, 15–16, 18–19, 24, 50–1, 80–1, 103–14, 127, 145
agency 9, 59
alienate 32
alienation 93
allegory, allegorical 67, 94, 99, 113
ally 32, 50
anger 1–2, 5–6, 17, 23–8, 31–9, 41–2, 55, 64, 125

angry 6, 28, 31–4, 36–42, 63, 68–9
Anglican 39, 62, 133, 136
anoint, anointed 40, 101, 108
anorexia 119
anxiety 87, 92, 110, 123
apartheid 64
apocalyptic 52
apophatic 54–5
Aquinas, Thomas 37–8, 42, 44
Aristotle 31
ascended 102
ascent 78, 109
assault 10, 32, 50, 60, 71, 91
atonement 102, 109
Augustine 36–7, 42, 89
autoimmune 12

Baldwin, Jennifer 145–6
Balthasar, Hans Urs von 102–3, 111
baptism 115
Beguines 118
Benedictine 94
benediction 2
bereavement 30
Bernard of Clairvaux 66, 99
Beste, Jennifer 81, 86
blame 9, 68
bless, blessing 40, 108, 113, 122, 126
Bonaventure 37
boundaries 6, 17, 123
brain 10, 12, 26, 84

147

bread 113, 115, 135, 142
breasts 117
breath, breathe 41, 71, 92, 110, 113, 134
 breathwork 11
burnout 125

Calvin 89, 98
cancer 92
capitalism 107
Carmelite 78
Carthusian 76,
Catholic 72, 102, 128
celibate 89
Celtic 144
charismatic 43
charity 43, 59
Christ 4, 15, 40, 44–5, 51–2, 54, 64, 94–5, 103, 114, 118–19, 126, 128, 135, 137–42
Christus Victor 102
Church 11, 14, 17, 19, 43, 48, 71, 74, 89, 93, 104, 127, 129–30, 137, 142, 144
Cistercian 99
cleanliness, cleanse 41, 87
clitoral 92
clothing, clothe 27, 67, 88
Cloud of Unknowing, The 76–7, 85
cognitive 22, 26, 80, 82, 120
colonial 52–3
comfort 5, 24, 27, 41, 70, 83, 135, 143,
 comfortable 5, 27, 39, 79, 134
community, communities 14, 30, 63, 67, 73, 75, 83, 85, 87, 107, 120–1, 131, 135, 145
companion 4, 7, 63, 72, 127, 145
compassion, compassionate 126, 135, 139, 145
condemn 36, 116
confession 4, 116, 130
conflict 32, 36, 69, 82
conscience 47, 55

consciousness 60, 65, 81
contemplation 31, 38, 71, 76, 77, 86, 113, 120, 122
contraception 89
conversion 38, 89
Corinthians 43, 67, 83
counselling 10, 21
creed 75, 80, 141
crucifix, crucifixion 16, 23, 40, 45, 51, 101, 103, 108, 130, 137, 143
cry 27, 38, 40, 54–5, 70, 77, 125, 141

dance 84, 98, 126, 132
darkness 76–8, 131–3, 136, 145–6
death 17, 26, 30, 37, 41, 44–5, 48–50, 51, 52, 70, 73, 78, 83, 88, 92, 101–5, 108–9, 126, 132, 137, 140, 141–2
decolonized 53
deconstruct 43, 73–5, 81, 83, 85, 125
demon 115
demonize 69
deny, denial 49, 51, 53, 119
depression 70, 92
deprivation 106, 111
Derrida, Jacques 24, 74, 76
descent, descend 102–3, 108–9, 111
desert 115
desire 14, 32, 36, 47, 65, 89, 94, 97, 104, 114, 118
despair 17, 23–4, 47, 64, 131
desperation 59
diet 115
Dionysius 54
disassociation 91, 96
discernment 38
disciple 5, 16, 52, 101–2, 106, 108, 131, 139
 discipleship 43
discipline 5, 16, 24

INDEX OF NAMES AND SUBJECTS

disconnect 91–2
disorientation 131, 136
doctrine 16, 49, 75, 80
dualism 88, 114
Dworkin, Andrea 71
dysregulation 93

Eagleton, Terry 48, 53, 57
Easter 16, 103–4, 111
eat, eating 2–3, 28, 108, 109, 112–13, 114, 115–25, 117–23
Ecclesiastes 64, 72, 126, 132
economic 35, 106–7
ecstatic 94, 117
endometriosis 59
endorphins 92
Ephesians 44, 83, 102
eros 95, 98–9
  erotic 65–6, 93–6, 99, 117–18
  eroticism 94
eschatological 43–7, 49, 51, 54, 56
esoteric, esotericism 95, 99
ethic 30, 35, 57, 107
  ethical 26, 47, 54–6, 88
Eucharist, eucharistic 81, 86, 114, 117–20, 123
Evangelical 29, 43, 74
  ExVangelical 74
evangelism 43
evensong 62
evil 40, 62, 73, 88, 106, 135, 143
exhaustion 27, 56, 59

faith 2, 14, 23, 29, 43, 45, 48–9, 59, 62, 64–5, 67, 73–87, 106, 108, 110, 134–5, 138, 142, 146
family 19, 26, 108, 120–1
fasting 2, 4, 112, 115–17, 119
fat 114–15, 123
fear 17, 74, 81–2, 93, 113, 131
feminist 34, 42, 63, 72, 123
fertile 69, 146
festivals 83, 116

flourish, flourishing 5, 12, 14, 20, 24, 50, 88
Foo, Stephanie 144, 146
forgive 5, 19–20, 21–4, 23–4, 28–9, 69, 131, 135, 143, 145
  forgiven 19
  forgiveness 1, 3, 5, 7, 19–26, 28–31, 42, 69
forsakenness 55, 104–5, 141
Foucault, Michel 53
Fowler, James 82–3, 86
fruit, fruitful 20, 69, 80, 84, 87, 113

Galatians 41
Galen 92
garden, gardening 84, 106
gaze 29, 63
gender 39, 90–1, 95, 107
Genesis 65, 88, 98, 105, 113
genitals 89
genocide 53
Gethsemane 106
glutton 114–15
grace 28, 44, 81, 86, 117, 122, 124, 132, 135–6, 138, 144, 145
gracious 143–4
greed 141
grief 17, 51, 80, 86, 108, 130, 132, 134, 139
guilty 93, 97, 120
gut 12, 83, 85
gynaecological 92

Hadewijch 117–18, 124
hallucinations 14, 52
harm 5, 15, 32, 34, 51, 68, 69, 125, 146
Harrowing of Hell 102–3
harvest 11
hate 27, 70, 126, 132
heal, healing 8, 23, 25, 60–1, 71, 98, 126, 132, 138, 140, 145–6
health 21, 27, 48, 71, 92–3

heaven 16, 38, 102, 113, 126, 132, 135, 142–3
Hegel 53, 57
hell 53, 102–3, 108–9, 111
heretic 85, 89
Herman, Judith 18
hierarchy 90, 115
hiking 84
holistic 93, 119
Holocaust 13, 57
Holy Saturday 16–17, 23, 28, 100–5, 108, 111, 129–31, 133, 137, 146
home 27, 58, 100, 106, 108, 139
homelessness 138
hope 2, 4, 10, 16, 20, 23, 43–57, 64, 72, 80, 84–5, 125, 127, 136–9, 142–4
  hopeless 2, 43, 45, 47, 49, 51–7, 54–6, 104, 125, 130
hormones, hormonal 10, 50, 92
hospitality 4, 58
humble 69
humiliation 116
hunger 116, 118, 122
hyperarousal 11
hypervigilant 10
hysteria 92

idols 73
Ignatius 111
illness 13, 106, 117
immortality 87–8
Incarnation, incarnate 4, 62, 114
infertility 59
Instagram 120, 122
intercession 49, 71, 144–5
  intercessor 141
intercourse 65–6, 88–91
Isaiah 3, 56
Isherwood, Lisa 114–15, 123
isolation 14, 78, 116
Israel, Israelite 56, 65

Jeremiah 47

Jerusalem 30, 63, 133, 141
Jewish 26, 30, 95, 109
Job 26, 41, 51, 58, 64, 69–70, 80, 100, 105, 108, 112
Jonah 41
Judges 106

kiss 65–6, 87, 94–5
Kolk, Bessel van der 10, 12, 18, 57

lament 64, 68, 140–2
Lamentations 64–5, 138, 142
Laub, Dori 13, 18
Lent 146
Leviticus 65, 88
liberation, liberated 13, 34, 47, 55, 60, 107, 127, 145
limbic system 10
Lorde, Audre 31, 33–4, 42, 96, 99

Magdalene, Mary 137, 139
Magnificat 62–3
Malachi 98
Manichaean 89
manna 113
masculinity, masculine 90, 107
masturbate 87–93, 92, 96–8
Maundy Thursday 130
meditation 40–2
memory 12, 15, 25–6, 29, 120–3, 145
mercy 40, 131, 138
Methodist 19
miracles 145
miscarriage 52
Moltmann, Jürgen 44–5, 57
monastic 99
Moses 55
mourn 27, 126, 132, 141–2
mystic 54, 76, 78, 81, 86, 94–5, 99, 103, 115–18
mysticism 81, 86, 94, 99

INDEX OF NAMES AND SUBJECTS

negation 74, 76
neglect 62
neoliberal 35
neoplatonic 88
neurodivergence 13
nightmares 13, 52
nourishment 34
Nussbaum, Martha 25, 31–2, 34, 36, 42

oil 65, 116–17
Onan 88–9
oppression 33–4, 36, 53, 104
optimism 46, 48, 51, 55, 57
orgasm 89, 90–3, 94, 97, 98, 118
Origen 66
oxytocin 92

patience 44, 113, 135
patriarchy 60, 64, 107
pedagogical 46, 76,
penis 89–91
penitence 131, 138
perpetrator 20, 38
persist, persistence 26, 77, 103, 105
phallocentric 90–1, 97–8
physiology 50, 124
Pilate 101, 133
pilgrimage 6–7
Plato 115
politics 4, 42
  political 18, 32, 42, 59, 63
poverty 47, 106
power 28, 31–2, 33, 56, 58, 61, 62, 68–72, 74, 96, 99, 101, 103, 110, 119, 134, 135, 143, 145
  powerless 56, 142
preach 109
  preachers 72, 104
pregnant 51, 90, 95, 118
priest 76, 101, 119
prophetic 34, 38, 62, 104
prostitution 89

protest 2, 58–72, 94, 125
Protestant 35, 107
Proverbs 64–5, 106
providence 47, 49, 54, 80
psychiatry 10, 18
  psychiatrist 12–13
psychology 3, 29, 50, 57, 71, 98–9
psychoanalysis 18
psychological 9–10, 20–1, 23–4, 26, 60, 93, 106
psychotherapy 10
psychosocial 106, 124
psychosomatic 38
PTSD 60, 124
purgation 78, 81, 83
purity 65, 87, 91–2

racism 33, 64, 107
Rambo, Shelly 16, 18, 50, 52, 57, 100, 103–5, 111
rape 66
reconciliation 5, 45, 75, 141
recovery 8, 18, 60
redeem 26, 35, 85
  Redeemer 39
Reformation 95
remaining 16, 18, 57, 70, 82, 103, 105, 111
reorientation 79
repair 26, 28, 30
resilience 48, 113
  resiliency 60
Resurrection 16–17, 44–5, 48–52, 57, 101–4, 109
revenge 21, 32–3
rituals 112
Rohr, Richard 83, 86
Romans 44, 46–7, 50
rosary 31, 39–42
Rupert of Deutz 94–5

sabbath 101–2, 105, 108–10
sacrifice 31, 91
salvation 35, 44, 51–5, 139, 145

Satan 26, 51
Saviour 102, 141-2
semen 88-90
servant 19, 55
sex 19, 65, 88-93, 95-6,
  sexual 22, 32, 57, 60, 65, 71,
    81, 87-93, 95-8, 111, 119
  sexuality 90-1, 93-9
shame 46, 61, 65, 68, 114
sin 5, 19-20, 28, 31, 36-8, 42,
  52, 87-8, 90, 98, 115-16, 131,
  138, 140
  sinful 24, 36, 87, 89-90, 97,
    114
slavery 47, 63
sleep 42, 70, 100, 105-11
Socrates 115
solace 132, 135, 145
solidarity 45, 48, 55, 105
Song of Songs 63-8, 87, 94
soul 21, 47, 63, 69-70, 75-6,
  78-9, 81, 94, 115, 125, 138,
  140, 145
spirituality 66-7, 81, 85, 93-7,
  99-100, 124, 127, 146
swimming 84
symbol 114, 130, 137

Taizé 133
taste 28, 117, 124
Teresa of Avila 78, 125, 128
testimony 25, 32, 46
thanksgiving 120, 143
therapy 3, 10, 12
tomb 57, 101, 108, 111, 135,
  137, 142
Torre, Miguel de la 51-3, 55, 57
toxic 47, 49
transcendence 82-3
transformation 18, 21, 57, 60, 91
transgression 22-3
  transgressions 29, 123
Trinity 39, 109, 141

triumph 44
triumphal 46, 48, 51-2, 103-4,
  109
Tutu, Archbishop Desmond 69

unclean 88-9, 108
Underhill, Evelyn 81-2, 86
unforgiveness 2-3, 19-27,
  29-30, 125
unhealthy 55, 87
utopia 53

vagina 89-91
Vatican 111
vernacular 76
victim 5, 13, 19, 21-2, 25, 36,
  57, 86, 111
victory 16-17, 28, 52, 61, 104,
  108
Vietnam 63, 71
violated 10, 50
  violation 36, 88
virginity 65

war 11, 63, 93, 126, 132
Ware, Kallistos 73, 85
weary 56, 96, 100, 105, 108,
  127
Weber, Max 35, 107
wisdom 20, 64-5, 83-4, 98, 113,
  117, 145-6
witness 13, 18, 24, 27, 105, 132
  witnessed 13-14, 27, 52
  witnessing 18, 52, 105, 108
womanist 63
worship 4, 49, 72, 112-13,
  129-30, 137, 144
worth, worthy 9, 16, 21-2, 28,
  35, 37, 60, 116, 119
  worthless 35
wounds 138, 140, 145

yoga 11, 84

www.ingramcontent.com/pod-product-compliance
Lightning Source LLC
Chambersburg PA
CBHW022016290426
44109CB00015B/1185